P9-BBP-830

Good Recipes
for
Hard Times

Good Recipes

for

Hard Times

LOUISE NEWTON

HOUGHTON MIFFLIN COMPANY BOSTON

1975

For my husband

whose enthusiasm, appreciation and discrimination
have made cooking three times a day
a joy for twenty-four years

Copyright © 1975 by Louise Newton. All rights reserved.
No part of this book may be reproduced or transmitted
in any form by any means, electronic or mechanical, including photocopying and recording, or by any information
storage or retrieval system, without permission in writing
from the publisher.

Library of Congress Cataloging in Publication Data

Newton, Louise.
    Good recipes for hard times.

    Includes bibliographical references and index.
    1. Cookery.   I. Title.
TX652.N42   641.5′52   75-15712
ISBN 0-395-20721-5   ISBN 0-395-21898-5 pbk.

Printed in the United States of America

c 10 9 8 7 6 5 4 3 2 1

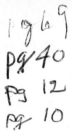

1969
pg 40
pg 12
pg 10

Preface

How can anybody think she knows enough to tell anybody, much less people struggling to survive on very low incomes, with all the extra problems that brings, how to cook their food? Well, I don't know, but I grew up in the Depression, the daughter of a minister, and I have seen food stretched pretty far. Also, I have gone on some expeditions with my husband when we had to live on a shoe-string, and cooking conditions were strange and minimal. And I love to cook (I've cooked for six for fifteen years), and to read cookbooks, and I have systematically searched out cheap ways to cook cheap things and still "set a good table."

Therefore, after being appalled, over and over, by what I saw people I knew to be on a tiny budget eating, by how much they were spending and how little pleasure they were getting out of it, I decided I'd like to see if I could put anything together that would help people please their palate as well as their budget.

There are a lot of books on how to cut costs in food. They are very good if you want to cut down from astronomical to a budget nearly twice as much as mine. But for getting well below that, the books I have seen are fearfully depressing, or not really very practical, or both. Some have you using fillers and stretchers so much that you can't imagine the food tasting like anything, and some list ingredients to go along with hamburger so expensive that you might as well have bought steak to begin with.

When I thought back about the good things I grew up with, like batter bread, and corn pudding, and molasses pie, and remembered some of the simple things I'd had elsewhere, like split pea soup in New England, and chicken and dumplings (in a college dining hall where you could get breakfast for 11¢!), and then things like egg and lemon soup (Greek) and polenta (Italian) and fried rice

(Chinese or Japanese) — it seemed to me there were enough simple, classic dishes in the world to make up a delicious diet on very, very little money.

Another thing that struck me as I read hundreds of recipes was that so many of the fanciest dishes were really just ingenious ways to use leftovers. Leftovers have been sadly neglected by most of the people I know. Of course leftovers can be perfectly horrible if they are not treated right. But I can remember when our Sunday roast went through a regular progression, ending with croquettes or hash or both, things that with proper treatment are perfectly delicious. And I remember the Brunswick stew we usually had right after we had chicken salad. The best parts of the hen went into the salad, and the rest into the stew. Both were divine. So I have indicated various good things to do with leftovers, in most cases right after the recipe for the original dish.

I have had in mind two somewhat different groups of people: First, people with almost no income whether on the long or short haul. Students and a lot of others find themselves in that position from time to time. The author certainly has. I had in mind that this first group would work out of the chapter "Hard Times," with excursions into the rest of the book as money permits. I also think anybody trying to keep his food budget really down will find the book useful, both because of the cheapness of the dishes, and of the reduction of waste as suggested in its pages. And the food, if I do say so, is good.

The guiding principle in this book then has been that everything should be delicious in its own right. I have also tried to keep out things that are too troublesome, and I have tried to pay attention to the requirements of nutrition, especially in the chapter "Hard Times," but always bearing in mind that the cook's first duty, and greatest pleasure, is to give people (including himself!) something to look forward to, three times every day.

Contents

Good Recipes
for
Hard Times

Hard Times

****

WHEN TIMES are really hard, it is all the more important to have your meals something everybody will look forward to. Three nice things happening every day will cheer up the grimmest of circumstances. I learned this for myself during exams when I was at school, where fortunately we had very good food. That this can be done with almost no money is apparent when you consider the delicious food eaten by the poorest people in areas that have a tradition of good cooking.

The recipes in this chapter, then, are all for good things to eat, welcome no matter how much money you may have. They also are all genuine recipes. They have not been altered to make them less expensive. But they meet two other requirements particularly pressing when money is very short: first you must fill your people up, and then you must give them the best nutrition possible with the money you have. This would be discouraging except that these requirements have been there for a lot of people since the beginning of time, and things like the rice of the Chinese, the pasta and polenta of the Italians, lentils from the Middle East, not to mention "Hopping John" of the Carolinas, or New England Kedgeree, are all examples of the wonderful dishes people have come up with. They all come down to starches, with the addition of whatever else was available.

This section of the cookbook, therefore, is divided into four main parts, one for each of the four main starches for our purpose: beans, rice, corn and wheat (more about the protein content of these later). There are a lot of potato recipes in this book, but potatoes are so expensive now that I have put the recipes for them in the vegetable section instead of here.

The most basic recipes for each starch are printed in this

chapter. At the end of each section of basic recipes I refer you to other recipes later in the book that do call for more expensive items. The point of all this is that you should always have beans, rice, cornmeal and grits (both from corn), and flour in your kitchen. Then what?

Protein. The most expensive thing you need in order to have good nutrition is protein. The nutrition experts say that if you drink a quart of milk a day you have more than half the protein you need. The best way to do this is to buy powdered milk (many doctors say it is better for you than whole milk).

The less money you have, the more important it is to have that milk. In a pinch, you can get all the rest of the protein you need from the staples mentioned above; see the budgets for particulars, pp. 133–141. The recipes in this chapter are ones you can use with just these ingredients, with a very few, mostly inexpensive, things added. See, for example, Portuguese Red Bean Soup, Lentils with Rice or Batter Bread.

If you wish, you can vary the milk with other dairy products. An ounce of cheese is about equivalent to a glass of milk in protein and doesn't cost a great deal more. And one egg contains as much protein as two thirds of a glass of milk; eggs are the next best buy to milk, I think, because they combine well with cheap things to make delicious dishes. Cheese does this too, but to a lesser extent. Milk, cheese, and eggs are all animal protein, the kind we need most. A good rule of thumb is to have enough of them to give us two thirds of the protein we need for the day. The rest can be gotten from the four basic starches above. There are notes further on in the chapter about the best way to combine these to get the most complete protein.

Other Needs. Of course protein, though the most expensive of the nutrition needs, is not the only one. You will want to add as much meat to your diet as you can afford, because we all like it, and also because it is a good source for many other important requirements like iron (fish is a good substitute for meat here). And vegetables and fruits must be included as often as you can for vitamins and minerals. The best thing to do, of course, is to eat as well-balanced a diet as possible. But let me emphasize again that when times are really hard, meals will have to be built around the starches, adding first the proteins you need to complement them, and then other things as you can. Read over the recipes in this chapter and you will begin to see how to add milk, eggs, cheese and vegetables to the best combination of starches, to make a balanced diet.

I have included four budgets with shopping lists and menus to go with them. Two are for emergency low budgets, less than half of the money suggested by the U.S. Department of Agriculture as necessary in their lowest economic bracket. The third is a budget for ordinary times, still much lower than the government's lowest budget, and the fourth for a retired couple living on Social Security. The emergency lists speak for themselves. To anyone on such a small budget, working up to any kind of variety would be very slow and there should be no need for anyone to stay on it long. However, they do include food that is adequate for a short haul, with lots of things that are good to eat, though repetitious. The other two budgets may take a bit of ingenuity in stretching the meat, but with good management you can make it go a long, long way (see pp. 61–62 on this) and they provide a generous amount of food that is so good that I don't think you'll get many complaints from the people you cook for.

Buying. Good management means thinking ahead and planning ahead. Suppose your budget is based on the earnings of one person making the minimum wage. See to it that you have spices, seasonings and herbs on hand all the time. If your income is variable, buy them when you are flush. If it is steady, think in terms of allotting perhaps 50¢ a week to them. Grow as many herbs as you can. Many can be grown in window boxes, and some, like thyme, chives, mint and basil, will grow indoors. All measurements of parsley are for dried parsley. Unless you can grow your own, fresh parsley will be too expensive.

Another important thing to do is to work toward buying staples in large quantities. Ten pounds of a store brand of rice will take a slice out of your budget, but it will provide the backbone of 20 meals for four people. Obviously you don't want to have all those meals in one week. But if you buy 10 pounds of rice one week, 10 of flour another week, 10 of cornmeal another week and so forth, you will be able to afford them, and you will always have them on hand.

You will notice in the pages on budgets that they include such ongoing items as starches, fats and spices. Even the first emergency budget includes a small can of curry powder. Careful stockpiling is what will turn groceries into satisfying meals. Most of your money will go on the proteins and starches, but a gradual process of collecting herbs, spices and other seasonings is just as important in turning out delicious meals.

Eggs and Cheese. I have added a supplementary section to this chapter in two parts: egg recipes and cheese recipes. Since eggs are at present one of the very cheapest ways to get animal protein, milk being the only other contender, eggs belong in any chapter on hard times.

Cheese, while nutritious, is on the other hand relatively expensive now, but this may not last. And in any case these recipes do not call for much cheese. There are other reasons for including it too: it keeps well, can be bought in small amounts without increasing the price per pound and is another good source of animal protein.

Vegetables and Fruit. I have been a bit discouraging about vegetables and fruit, but it is important to remember that *some* must be included every week. Again there are two things to bear in mind: what you can afford, and what will add the most to your basic dishes or menu. In the late spring, summer and early fall there are many delightful vegetables which can be bought without ruining the budget, or better still grown in your own yard. But in the winter there are cabbages and carrots. Of course there are frozen and canned vegetables, and they should play their part in your diet. But cabbages and carrots are the real standbys. Between the two of them you get most of the vitamins you need from vegetables, though they should be supplemented, especially with the dark green vegetables, like turnip greens, kale, mustard greens and collards. I've included as many recipes as I could for cabbage and carrots, some of which could be the backbone of lunch or supper. The other vegetable that appears frequently is tomato. Except when you can get fresh ones cheaply this means canned tomatoes. If you don't cook them too long, tomatoes are a good source of vitamin C and canning does not destroy this. But the main virtue of the tomato for our purpose is what it does for other dishes. A simple tomato sauce makes polenta (cornmeal mush), for example, delicious, and you can make nearly a whole meal between the two of them. An addition of cheese, grated and put on top, would make this a nourishing and well-balanced lunch or supper for four. (See recipe, p. 21.)

About fruit I can only say that the one fruit I can fit into my budget, except for special occasions, is the ordinary Florida orange, which I find at a very reasonable price at one of the markets I go to. This may reflect some personal prejudice, but in any case I expect to provide most of the needed vitamins and minerals with vegetables. I might add, though, that when I do find fruits at a good price in season, I grab them.

So if times are hard, start with the starches and then buy your milk. Everything else you buy should contribute toward making good dishes and good meals out of the starches. There is such a variety of delicious recipes for these, there is no excuse for dreary meals however small your budget may be.

Beans

Beans are an excellent source of protein, which as we have seen is the most expensive need that has to be met. However, it is not a complete protein, the kind you get from meat, or eggs, or milk and other dairy foods. In order to make it complete, which is necessary for good nutrition, you must add things at the same meal that will fill it out. There is a table on p. 132 showing how to do that but, very simply speaking, if you add corn, or something made from corn like cornmeal muffins, to your meal the protein value of the beans will be greatly increased. The same is true if you add other starches like rice or spaghetti. If you add a glass of milk to this you will really be in business.

You will notice that many of the recipes in this section call for combinations like those suggested above. It is fascinating to me that long before the science of nutrition was born the Indians had discovered succotash and the Italians beans and pasta — there are numberless examples of traditional recipes that meet this requirement, or come close to it.

Cooked Beans

Many recipes call for cooked beans. The simplest thing to do is to boil them according to the following recipe. If what you are making does not call for the water they were cooked in, save it to use as the basis for a soup.

1 pound dried beans	⅛ teaspoon thyme
water to cover plus 2 inches	2 cloves
1 onion, whole	1 bay leaf
1 clove garlic	2 teaspoons salt
1 tablespoon parsley	pepper

All beans should be rinsed quickly before using. Soak most beans overnight in the water unless the package suggests otherwise. (Lentils and split peas do not need to be soaked.) Next day put beans and water in which they were soaked in a pot, add all the rest of the ingredients and simmer until tender. Most beans will cook in about 2 hours, though some brands have been treated for shorter cooking times and if so the package will specify the cooking time. Exceptions to the 2-hour rule are lentils (30 to 40 minutes), split peas (the same), cream peas (about 1 hour) and perhaps others. (Actually I expect all these have been treated too, but if so I have never seen the untreated kinds.)

If you want to cook beans and have forgotten to soak them, cover them with boiling water plus 2 inches, and let them stand an hour before cooking.

New England Baked Beans

1 pound dried navy beans	1 teaspoon salt
¼ to ½ pound bacon (seasoning bacon, ends and pieces, are good for this) or salt pork	⅓ cup molasses
	1 cup boiling water
1 teaspoon mustard	more boiling water, enough to cover beans
2 teaspoons sugar	

Soak beans overnight. Next day drain beans and bring soaking water to a boil. Put the mustard, sugar and salt into a bowl and blend. Add 1 cup of the boiling water and the molasses to the mustard mixture. Put beans and pork in alternate layers in a heavy baking pot. Pour the mustard and molasses mixture over the beans and pork and add enough additional boiling water to come to the top of the pot's contents.

Bake covered at about 250° (see directions on package of beans; if no time is given it means the beans have not been treated for quicker cooking and they will have to cook 6 to 8 hours — you may want to substitute Great Northern beans which will cook in 2 to 2½ hours). Add more boiling water if needed during baking period. The beans should be covered with the juice.

Baked Bean Soup

⅔ cup leftover baked beans,
   cooked as above
1 large onion, coarsely chopped
2 tablespoons margarine or other
   fat
2 medium potatoes, peeled and
   sliced

2 teaspoons parsley
salt and pepper
3 cups water
3 cups milk (add extra margarine
   if nonfat milk is used)

Sauté onion in margarine until soft. Add potatoes, baked beans, parsley, salt and pepper and water. Simmer covered until everything is very soft, 30 to 45 minutes. Put this through a sieve, add milk, taste for seasoning, reheat and serve.

Fried Leftover Baked Beans

Put the beans, liquid and all, on a plate. Sprinkle on enough cornmeal to take up the liquid. Mix this up and then mash with a fork. Shape into patties and fry in hot fat. Bacon grease is best if you have some on hand; use just enough to cover the pan to perhaps ⅛-inch depth. Fry on both sides until brown.

Beans in Oil

This is a delicious and different way to cook beans. It is best if cooked with beans that won't get too mushy, such as chickpeas, crowder peas, or cream peas, but any beans will do. Red kidney beans and pinto beans would be my last choice.

1 pound dried beans, cooked (p. 6)	3 or 4 large onions, sliced and halved
¼ cup or more oil	1 tablespoon paprika

Sauté onions and paprika in oil until soft. Add cooked and drained beans and stir gently until heated through and flavors are blended. This makes a large quantity, but since it is good either hot or cold (room temperature is best of all), you will have no trouble using it up. This dish is best with lots of oil, lots of onion and lots of paprika.

Beans and Pasta

This is one of my very favorite things to eat. It is very hearty, quite highly seasoned, and the proportions given will feed six hungry people. If you don't like garlic, it is worth learning to like it just for this dish.

Below are given the basic ingredients, but they may vary in proportion according to taste, or what you have on hand, and almost anything in the refrigerator (except green peas) may be added to it: leftover beef, chicken, snap beans, baby limas, corn, okra, squash (this is particularly good), chicken or beef stock, or gravy. Just be sure you have beans, pasta, and as much garlic as you can take.

1½ cups dried Great Northern beans, or other beans	1 tablespoon parsley
	⅛ teaspoon thyme
4 tablespoons bacon grease, or salt pork, tried out	bay leaf
	1 clove
3 stalks celery with leaves	2 teaspoons salt
2 large onions, chopped	red pepper
4 cloves garlic, mashed	1 cup raw pasta, any kind
4 cups water or stock (use soaking water)	

Rinse beans quickly, and soak them overnight if necessary (see directions p. 6). Sauté celery, onions and garlic in fat until soft. Add all the rest of the ingredients except the pasta. Simmer covered about 2 hours, or until beans are about done. Add pasta and simmer 20 minutes longer (5 minutes longer than package directions — pasta should be soft). Serve in soup bowls. You may put a piece of toast in each bowl before putting in the beans and pasta.

Bean Soup (Greek Fassoulada)

1 cup dried lima beans, or other beans
4 cups water (use soaking water)
1 stalk celery, chopped
1 carrot, quartered and sliced
1 large onion, coarsely chopped
2 heaping teaspoons tomato paste
1 tablespoon parsley
4 tablespoons oil
salt and pepper

Rinse beans quickly and soak them overnight if necessary (see directions p. 6). Put beans and water into soup pot and simmer covered until just done. If beans are untreated it will take about 2 hours but you had better watch them. When they are just done, add the rest of the ingredients and simmer all together about 30 minutes longer.

Black-eyed Peas

A standby in the South. Cooked with rice it is called "Hopping John." It is very good.

1 pound dried black-eyed peas
water to cover with 2 inches to spare
4 slices bacon, or equivalent in ends and pieces, or salt pork
2 teaspoons salt
1 tablespoon parsley
⅛ teaspoon thyme
pepper
bay leaf
2 cloves
1 onion, quartered
1 large clove garlic
¼ cup raw long-grain rice (optional)

Rinse black-eyed peas quickly and soak them overnight. Next day put water and peas into a large pot. Add the rest of the ingredients except the rice and simmer, covered, 2 to 3 hours. Most of the water should boil away. If you wish you may add rice for the last 30 minutes of cooking. There should be about enough liquid for the rice to take up. Add more boiling water if necessary.

Lentils with Rice

12 ounces dried lentils	2 tablespoons margarine
water to cover with 1 inch to spare	salt and pepper
1 to 2 onions, sliced	½ cup rice

Rinse lentils quickly and soak overnight if necessary (probably not, but see directions p. 6). Put lentils on to boil in cold water. Add onions, which you have sautéed in the margarine until soft, and salt and pepper. Simmer about 40 minutes (see package directions). Twenty minutes before lentils are ready, add the rice. The rice should just about take up the liquid (see directions in Boiled Rice II, p. 13, for managing this). This is best seasoned with only salt and pepper in addition to the onion and margarine.

Lentil Salad

1 cup dried lentils	2 teaspoons parsley
4 cups water	⅛ teaspoon thyme
1 onion, left whole	1 teaspoon salt
1 clove	pepper
1 clove garlic	French dressing
small bay leaf	made with garlic

Simmer lentils in water with all the seasonings about 30 minutes (see package directions — they probably do not need soaking). They should be cooked through but not soft. Drain and chill, saving liquid for soup another day. Toss in the dressing lightly, so as not to break up lentils. Serve cold or at room temperature (better). Delicious.

Lentil Soup

1 pound dried lentils	2 onions, quartered
2 quarts water	4 stalks celery, cut up
2 cloves garlic, mashed	3 tablespoons oil
2 teaspoons vinegar	small bay leaf, if liked

Rinse lentils quickly and cook all ingredients together until very soft (add 10 minutes to package directions for lentils, probably about 40 minutes — lentils generally do not need soaking). Put through sieve, reheat and serve.

Portuguese Red Bean Soup

1 cup dried red kidney beans
1 large onion, coarsely chopped
2 cloves garlic, mashed
3 tablespoons bacon grease or
    other fat
1 6-ounce can tomato paste with
    5 cups water, or substitute
    (such as canned tomatoes with
    less water)

3 bay leaves
scant ½ teaspoon ground allspice
pinch of thyme leaves
salt and pepper
4 medium potatoes, peeled and
    cut into roughly ¾-inch chunks

Rinse beans quickly and soak overnight if necessary (see directions p. 6). Sauté onions and garlic in bacon grease or substitute until soft. Add beans to this, along with tomato and water (use water the beans were soaked in). Add bay leaves, allspice, thyme, salt and pepper. Simmer, covered, at least 1¼ hours. Then add potatoes and simmer 45 minutes more. Taste for seasoning. Let stand a few minutes before serving.

Beans and Rice

Many kinds of beans, either dried or canned, are good with rice. Rice may be added to beans toward the end of boiling as for Black-eyed Peas (p. 9). Or the rice may be cooked as a pilaff (p. 14), and drained cooked or canned beans added with the liquid. The simplest and quickest way is to boil rice as in Boiled Rice I (p. 13). While that is boiling, onions, garlic or both should be sautéed in margarine in a large frying pan or casserole. When rice is done, add it to the onions or garlic in the margarine, toss well, add drained cooked or canned beans, toss again, heat through and serve. This is my favorite way. All make an excellent and nutritious (and quick) lunch.

Note: If using canned beans drain and rinse them very carefully or the dish will taste "canned." If using beans you have cooked, save the liquid to use as a basis for soup on a later day.

Tio Pepe

1 cup dried beans, red kidney or
   other
2 tablespoons oil
1 teaspoon salt
pepper

½ whole bulb of garlic
2 slices bacon, or ends and pieces
1 clove garlic, mashed
¼ teaspoon ground cumin

Rinse beans quickly and soak overnight if necessary (see directions p. 6). Put beans, soaking water and oil in a pot, season with 1 teaspoon of salt, and pepper, and add the garlic without peeling the cloves. Simmer until done, about 1½ to 2 hours. Drain beans, saving liquid and garlic for use in soup later. Meanwhile cut the bacon in 1-inch pieces and sauté until crisp and brown, pouring off excess fat and adding mashed garlic for the last minute or two. Add the beans and the cumin and mix well. Keep on very low heat until flavors are blended, about 15 minutes.

Split Pea Soup

1 pound dried split peas
2 quarts boiling water
bay leaf

3 to 4 cloves garlic, mashed
3 whole cloves
2 teaspoons salt

Add peas slowly enough to the boiling water to keep it boiling. Add bay leaf, garlic, cloves and salt. Simmer, covered, 1 to 2 hours. It is better with longer cooking. This soup is delicious just as it is, but you may add onion, carrots and celery, first sautéed in margarine, 15 minutes before serving.

Rice

There are a good many different kinds of rice, and as many ways of cooking it. From my experience, there seem to be in this country two main kinds of rice in ordinary supermarkets: the long grain and the medium grain. The medium grain is noticeably less expensive and does very well for the first method of boiling rice given below. To be good, rice should be dry and fluffy, with each grain separate, and medium-grain rice gets dry and fluffy when cooked as in Boiled Rice I. This method takes high heat for 15 to 20 minutes, however, and if you don't want to do that, use the second method with long-grain rice. Also the long-grain rice is better for pilaffs (or pilaus), for which several recipes are given below.

Don't be timid about cooking plain raw rice. The knack is very easily acquired and it is quick and easy to cook. And it is much cheaper, and in my opinion much better, than all the precooked or partially cooked kinds I have seen.

As in the bean section (see introduction, p. 5) many of these recipes include combinations of ingredients that help to make up complete proteins, whether with peas or beans, or with milk or eggs, or with some amount of meat or cheese added. As always, a glass of milk, made from powdered milk or not, served with the meal will just about make up the complete protein you need.

Boiled Rice I

1 cup raw rice   1 tablespoon salt
2 quarts water

Bring salted water to a rolling boil in a large pot (there should be 8 times as much water as rice — if you're cooking only a small amount of rice you won't need such a large pot; for ½ cup raw rice, 1 quart of water is sufficient). Add rice slowly so that water does not stop boiling. Boil rice over high heat, uncovered, 15 to 20 minutes, until it is done through. The time varies with the brand of rice and you will just have to taste it the first time you buy a new brand. When it is done, drain into a colander. Shake it to get all the liquid out. Have the oven warm. Put rice on a plate or flat dish, turn heat in oven off and set the rice in the oven for a few minutes to dry out.

Boiled Rice II

1 cup raw long-grain rice   1 teaspoon salt
2½ cups water

Bring salted water to a boil and add rice. When it returns to the boil, stir up once with a fork, reduce heat to low, and simmer, covered, *until done*. When it is done it will be dry and fluffy. This usually takes about 30 minutes. Until you are familiar with cooking rice, and also with your burners, check it often after about 20 minutes. If it is running dry and rice is not done, add more boiling water. If, on the other hand, it is done, but the liquid has not boiled away, turn up the heat a *little*, and cook with the top off until the water has gone.

Rice Pilaff

The basic difference between rice pilaff and plain rice is that the rice is sautéed gently in margarine and then cooked in stock or water. Even with this simplest kind a little onion is generally sautéed in the margarine first.

1 cup raw long-grain rice	2 cups good chicken stock,
2 tablespoons margarine	or water
1 small onion, chopped fine	1 teaspoon salt

Sauté onions in margarine until soft. Add rice slowly and keep stirring around until all is added and rice is somewhat transparent. Add stock or water and salt. Simmer, covered, until rice is done (see Boiled Rice II, above). Use stock if it has a good flavor, and reduce salt. If you use water, color and flavor will be improved if you add a little turmeric (be careful) and if you sauté a bit of mashed garlic along with the onions.

Arroz à la Cubana

1 cup raw rice	2 to 3 tablespoons margarine
2 cloves garlic, left whole	poached or fried eggs
2 cloves garlic, mashed	

Cook rice in a lot of water (see Boiled Rice I) with the whole garlic cloves. Drain and dry in oven. Sauté mashed garlic in margarine slowly while rice is cooking. Add drained rice and toss and cook a few minutes. Serve with fried or poached eggs on top.

Baked Rice

1½ cups cold boiled rice	2 tablespoons margarine,
1 egg, beaten	melted
1 cup milk	¼ teaspoon salt

Beat up egg in a mixing bowl. Add the rest of the ingredients and mix well. Pour into a baking dish and cook at a low temperature (300°) until set, about an hour. It should be a nice golden brown.

Chow Farn

4 cups boiled rice, cold
2 medium onions, coarsely chopped
2 tablespoons oil

2 eggs
salt to taste
1 tablespoon soy sauce

Sauté onions in oil until soft, and add eggs beaten with salt. Stir constantly until just set. Then add rice and soy sauce and mix quickly. This is delicious, and even more so if you have green onions, or sprouts from old onions. Just chop them and add raw with the rice instead of the sautéed onions, and add eggs directly to heated oil.

Curried Rice

1 cup raw rice
2 tablespoons bacon grease or substitute
1 large onion, coarsely chopped
1 green pepper, coarsely chopped, *or* 2 tablespoons parsley
1½ teaspoons curry powder, or to taste

⅛ teaspoon thyme leaves
1 teaspoon salt
1 cup canned tomatoes, or substitute (see p. 130)
2 cups stock (may be made with bouillon cubes)
crumbled crisp bacon (optional)

Sauté onion in fat until soft, and also green pepper if used. (This is good with the green pepper if it is cheap, but parsley makes an excellent substitute.) Add the rice gradually and stir until it is somewhat transparent, add other ingredients and cook as for plain rice pilaff (p. 14).

Green Rice

2 cups boiled rice
1 egg
1 cup milk
1 small onion, chopped fine
2 tablespoons oil

2 tablespoons parsley
salt to taste
½ cup grated cheese, preferably Muenster or Brick

Beat up egg; add milk and stir. Add all other ingredients and mix. Bake in 350° oven about 40 to 45 minutes, until set. Double this recipe and you will have nearly a whole meal for four hungry people.

Rice with Leftover Vegetables

1 cup raw long-grain rice
1 onion, coarsely chopped
1 clove garlic, mashed
2 to 3 tablespoons margarine
2½ cups water

1 to 1½ cups leftover vegetables, coarsely chopped
1 to 2 teaspoons parsley
salt and pepper

Green vegetables are especially good for this — snap beans, spinach, okra — but beans, corn and carrots would be good too. Let your common sense be your guide. I wouldn't want to include, for example, both okra and broccoli. This is a handy way to use up a lot of little dabs of vegetables, and it is very good. Adding cooked beans to this will make it more nutritious.

Sauté onion and garlic in margarine until soft. Add rice gradually and stir until it is somewhat transparent. Add other ingredients and cook as in rice pilaff (p. 14).

Rice Pancakes

1½ cups boiled rice
1 teaspoon soda
2 cups buttermilk

2 cups flour
½ teaspoon salt
1 to 2 eggs, beaten

Dissolve the soda in the buttermilk. Mash the rice. (This is a little bit troublesome but these pancakes are delicious and easily worth it. Mash in a metal mixing bowl with a wooden mallet if you have one, otherwise a fork will do.) Sift the flour and salt onto a plate. Work the beaten eggs into the rice. Then add flour mixture alternately with the buttermilk mixture and mix well. Cook on hot skillet as usual for pancakes (p. 31), but they will take a little longer, about 5 minutes in all, or 2½ minutes to a side.

Rice Pudding

This is the kind I grew up with and I like it much better than the "creamy" kinds most cookbooks offer. My husband, who has always hated rice pudding, likes this too.

3 cups boiled rice	2 cups milk
1 egg	nutmeg to taste
¼ teaspoon salt	3 tablespoons margarine,
⅓ cup sugar	melted

Beat up egg and salt together well. Add sugar and beat well again. Add milk and nutmeg and melted margarine and mix well. Add rice and mix well once more. Put in a greased baking dish and bake at 375° for 30 minutes, or until set.

Rice with Tomatoes and Okra

3 cups boiled rice	1 cup okra cut up (about ½ 10-
2 to 4 slices bacon, or ends and	ounce pkg. frozen or same
pieces, cut in 1-inch squares	amount fresh)
1 medium onion, coarsely chopped	salt and pepper
1 cup canned tomatoes, or	
substitute (see p. 132)	

Sauté bacon and onions in the fat from the bacon until brown. Add tomatoes, okra, salt and pepper. Simmer, partly covered, for 15 or 20 minutes, until the liquid has boiled down some. Add rice, stir once and simmer very slowly, still partly covered, until liquid is gone, about 10 minutes perhaps, but you will have to check it from time to time. This makes a whole meal.

Tomato Pilaff

1 cup raw long-grain rice	1 to 1½ cups canned tomatoes
2 slices bacon, or ends and pieces,	1½ cups water
cut to 1-inch squares	scant teaspoon salt
1 medium onion, coarsely	pepper
chopped	

Sauté bacon and onions in the fat from the bacon until brown. Reduce heat to low and add rice slowly, stirring until it becomes somewhat transparent. Add all other ingredients and cook as for rice pilaff (p. 14).

Note: This is really Red Rice (p. 86) in its simplest form. I have included it in this spot, however, because it is much cheaper, and also because it is delicious in its own right.

Cornmeal

Corn and cornmeal, when combined with things like milk or eggs, cheese or bits of meat, or with beans as in succotash, help to make up the complete protein we need each day. See the introduction to the bean section and the table on p. 132 for more on this. Yellow and white cornmeal can be used interchangeably.

Batter Bread I

1 cup yellow cornmeal
3 tablespoons margarine
1½ cups cold water
1½ teaspoons baking powder

1½ teaspoons salt
1½ cups milk (scant measure)
1 large or 2 small eggs

Put margarine and water in a small saucepan and bring to a boil. Sift together dry ingredients. Pour boiling water and margarine over the dry ingredients. Stir until batter swells up and is well mixed. Beat up egg(s) in a separate bowl and add milk. Pour this mixture very gradually into the cornmeal mixture, stirring constantly to prevent lumps (easy if you do it a little at a time). Pour into a greased baking dish and bake at 350° for 45 minutes. This makes a soft, delicious dish. Use two large eggs if you like it stiffer. I don't. This is one of my husband's and my favorite dishes.

Batter Bread II

This is very like the preceding one, but having more eggs in it makes it both more expensive and more nutritious. If you wish to serve it with just a vegetable or two and no meat, this is the one to serve.

1 cup yellow cornmeal
1 teaspoon baking powder
1½ teaspoons salt
1 tablespoon margarine

1½ cups water
3 eggs
1 cup milk

Mix and cook as for Batter Bread I.

Corn Bread I

1½ cups yellow cornmeal
¾ cup sifted flour
4 teaspoons baking powder
1 teaspoon salt

2 tablespoons sugar
2 eggs
1¼ cups milk
¼ cup melted shortening or oil

Sift together dry ingredients. Beat eggs in a separate bowl. Add milk and then add egg and milk mixture gradually to dry ingredients and beat until smooth. Add fat or oil and mix well. Bake in a greased baking dish at 400° for 30-35 minutes. (I don't bother to beat the eggs separately. I just add eggs, oil and milk to the sifted dry ingredients and mix the whole thing with a wire whisk. It's a lot easier, if you have a wire whisk.)

Corn Bread II

I like this even better than the above recipe, though it is not as hearty or as pretty.

1 cup white cornmeal
½ cup flour
1 teaspoon salt
2 teaspoons baking powder if fresh milk is used, or 1 teaspoon baking powder if sour milk or buttermilk is used
½ teaspoon soda, *only* if sour milk or buttermilk is used, in addition to 1 teaspoon baking powder

2 eggs
1 cup milk, fresh or sour, or buttermilk
3 tablespoons melted fat or oil

Mix as for Corn Bread I. Bake in a greased dish at 350° about 25 minutes.

Buttermilk Corn Bread

2 cups cornmeal	2 cups buttermilk
1 teaspoon salt	1 egg
¾ teaspoon soda	3 tablespoons oil or melted fat

Sift together cornmeal and salt. Dissolve soda in buttermilk. Combine all ingredients and mix well. Pour into a greased iron skillet and bake at 350° about 35 minutes.

Cornmeal Dabs

These are absolutely delicious. They are fine by themselves, or with grated cheese sprinkled on them, or with various sauces like those for polenta, or with syrup or honey. They are quickly made.

1 cup yellow cornmeal	¼ cup milk
1½ cups boiling water	1 teaspoon salt
1 tablespoon margarine	margarine for sautéing
1 egg	

Pour boiling water over cornmeal and margarine and stir until well mixed and swelled up. Beat up egg until light in a separate bowl; add milk and salt and mix well. Add egg-and-milk mixture gradually to cornmeal mixture, stirring after each addition to keep it from lumping. Heat frying pan over medium heat. Melt about 1 tablespoon margarine for each panful. Drop by tablespoons onto pan and cook on both sides until brown, about 4 minutes in all.

Hoecakes

These are the irreducible minimum, but I love them. We used to have them as children out in the deep country of North Carolina. I used to wish we could have them at home. They are good "baked" on a lightly greased frying pan as for pancakes, and served with margarine and molasses. They are *delicious* fried in bacon grease or some substitute. Cooked either way the ingredients are simply:

2 cups cornmeal	2 cups boiling water
1 teaspoon salt	bacon grease or other fat, if fried

Pour boiling water over cornmeal and salt. Stir until well mixed and swelled up. Leave to cool until you can shape it into cakes ½ to ¾ inch thick and about 3 inches in diameter. "Bake" as above. Or, heat fat in a heavy frying pan over medium high heat. The fat should be about ¼ inch deep in the pan. Fry cakes in hot fat until brown on both sides. Serve while crisp and hot. (Don't try to keep them hot more than a minute or two in the oven — they will get soggy.) Don't forget to put the molasses on the table.

Cornmeal Muffins

These are unbelievably good. Fine for company meals.

¾ cup yellow cornmeal	½ teaspoon soda
1 cup flour	2 eggs
2 teaspoons sugar	½ cup oil or melted fat
1 teaspoon salt	1 cup buttermilk
1 teaspoon baking powder	

Sift together dry ingredients into a bowl. Add eggs, oil and buttermilk. Mix well with a wire whisk or spoon. Pour into greased muffin tins and bake about 12 minutes at 400°. This makes about 12 muffins about 2 inches in diameter. They are good split and heated over with cheese on top if any are left.

Polenta

This almost deserves a chapter to itself. Polenta is one of nature's greatest gifts to the cook. It is dirt cheap even now. Polenta for six costs one quarter of what spaghetti for six costs. But like pasta, it is delicious with a great many different things, and is perhaps a little more versatile. Also like pasta, it is a staple in northern Italy. It is really nothing but cornmeal mush, allowed to set, and served with various accompaniments. Basic polenta is made from:

1 cup yellow cornmeal	1 teaspoon salt
3 cups water	

Put 2 cups water and the salt on to boil. Put cornmeal into a bowl and add 1 cup cold water gradually, stirring to keep it from lumping. Add cornmeal mixture gradually to the boiling water. Simmer, covered, about 30 minutes, opening up to stir often, until it is stiff.

You may use a double boiler for this if you wish. It is easier as it does not need stirring, but it takes longer. Bring the other 2 cups water to a boil in the top of a double boiler over direct heat. Add the cornmeal prepared as above and bring back to a boil, stirring constantly. Have water boiling in the bottom of the double boiler and put the top over it as soon as the cornmeal mixture boils. Cover the whole thing and cook about an hour.

When the polenta is cooked, pour it into a shallow pan or dish to cool. I like mine ⅜ to ½ inch thick. Serve in pie-shaped wedges like pizza, at room temperature, covered with one of the various accompaniments, which are served hot. Or cut it into desired shapes and sauté gently in margarine before serving, if you like it hot.

Accompaniments for Polenta

The list for these could be endless. Polenta is most often served with cheese in some way, or with some kind of tomato sauce, and I suggest several different ways below. These are just starters, however. Vegetables, leftover meats, fish or chicken, served in all manner of sauces, such as plain cream sauce, a cheese sauce, barbecue sauce, curry sauce, creole sauce — all would be good with it, and many others. Polenta may also be substituted for spaghetti, or for the bread base for pizza. You could go on and on.

Polenta with Grated Cheese
(and maybe Onion)

Cut polenta, cooked as above and cooled and set, into shapes and sauté gently in a film of oil and margarine mixed. Serve hot covered with grated cheese. It is delicious. Sliced onions sautéed in margarine until soft may be put on top of the cheese. Delicious too!

Creole Sauce for Polenta

1 stalk celery, chopped
1 large onion, coarsely chopped
½ green pepper, chopped
2 tablespoons margarine
1-pound can tomatoes
1 tablespoon parsley
good pinch ground cloves
salt and pepper

Sauté celery, onion and pepper until soft in margarine. Add canned tomatoes, juice and all, breaking up the tomato pieces. Add parsley, cloves, salt and pepper. Simmer, uncovered, about 30 minutes. If too much liquid is lost, add a little boiling water.

Ham Gravy and Peas over Polenta

Leftover ham gravy (see Ham, p. 85) may be used to good advantage over polenta. Add some canned tomatoes, about half as much as the gravy, or more if you like, and any leftover vegetables you may have. (Peas are particularly good for this.) Serve hot over polenta cooked as in general instructions.

Okra and Tomato Sauce for Polenta

2 slices bacon (ends and pieces) cut into 1-inch pieces
1 onion, coarsely chopped
1 cup canned tomatoes
½ 10-ounce pkg. frozen okra, or same amount fresh
salt and pepper

Sauté bacon. Add onion and sauté until soft. Add the rest of the ingredients and simmer about 30 minutes. Serve over polenta cooked as in general instructions.

Piedmont Sauce for Polenta

1 onion, chopped fine
1 clove garlic, mashed
2 tablespoons margarine
1½ teaspoons paprika
1½ to 2 cups canned tomatoes
salt and pepper

Sauté onion and garlic in margarine until soft. Add paprika and sauté a minute or two more. Add canned tomatoes, juice and all, and salt and pepper, and simmer until flavors are blended.

Grits, or Hominy Grits

Grits is (trouble, right there) a rather complicated subject, but important where I live. Everybody else will say, no doubt, "Why not forget it?" Well, though it is much like cornmeal to handle and at the same time less versatile, it does have some advantages, so we will press on. I don't know where the name comes from, really. I have read that it should be "grist" before cooking and "grits" after. It is also frequently called "hominy," which I suspect is the older name. At any rate it is corn treated with lye, and it is white. It comes in several sizes — I have seen it in three: (1) big hominy, the whole grain of the corn, which I am skipping for the simple reason that I don't like it (I have never seen many recipes for it — it comes only in cans as far as I know), (2) grits, or hominy grits, which is milled fine like cornmeal, and (3) a size in between which a friend from Florida gave me as a great treat and which I am ashamed to say I never did cook, and I have never seen any since.

From now on, then, we will be talking about hominy, or grits, milled fine. A lot of different things can be done with grits but unlike cornmeal it must always be boiled first (a procedure almost exactly the same as making cornmeal mush but easier). So, though cooked grits can be incorporated into breads, pancakes and so forth, it cannot really be used in baking like cornmeal.

On the other hand, it is easier to boil than cornmeal mush because it doesn't lump easily, and any lumps that do form are very quickly smoothed out. Also, unlike most things, the quick-cooking kind does perfectly well, though I like to cook it longer than the box says, 20 to 30 minutes. Another advantage is that it is ready to eat after boiling; in a pinch you can serve the quick-cooking kind in 10 or 15 minutes. Though other things may be done to it, it is very good just as it is. It sets hard when cold and slices easily for various uses.

Grits, or Hominy Grits

1 cup grits
1 teaspoon salt

5 cups boiling water (4 cups if cooked in double boiler)

Method 1. In a heavy pot bring water and salt to a boil and add grits, stirring constantly until it boils again. Simmer, covered, 25 to 30 minutes. Stir every 5 minutes or so, scraping up from the bottom (the lumps will disappear).

Method 2. Bring 4 cups of water to a boil in the top of a double boiler over direct heat. Bring 1½ inches of water to a boil in the bottom of the double boiler. Add grits and salt to the 4 cups water, bring back to a boil, stirring constantly, and then place the top pan over the bottom pan. Cover the whole thing and cook about 45 minutes, or more if you like it creamier — perhaps an hour. Stir once or twice if convenient, but basically this can just be left. Stir thoroughly before serving.

Serve with margarine or gravy. It is especially good with ham gravy or other pork gravy. (For ham gravy see Ham, p. 85.)

Baked Hominy Grits

1 cup grits, cooked (makes about 4 cups)	½ teaspoon salt
	pepper
½ cup milk	1 egg
2 tablespoons margarine	

Heat milk and margarine in an oven dish. Add cooked grits and salt and pepper. Mix well. Beat up egg in a separate bowl and incorporate (see p. 101) into the grits mixture. Bake at 350° about 30 minutes, until set and a little browned.

This is a minimum recipe and is very good. It is a little better with 2 eggs and more margarine. This needs no accompaniment and can be the biggest part of the meal.

Fried or Sautéed Hominy Grits

Put grits to cool in a container which will give it a nice shape for slicing. When you are ready to use it, cut slices about ⅜ inch thick. Dip the slices in milk — dredge in toast crumbs first if you wish — and sauté, or sauté them plain in margarine and serve with sauces or with gravy or with syrup. They are especially good plain if you sauté some onions in the margarine first, and heap the onions on top of the sliced and sautéed grits to serve.

Hominy Bread

2 cups cooked hominy grits	½ teaspoon salt
2 eggs	1 cup cornmeal
1 tablespoon oil or other fat, melted	1 scant tablespoon baking powder
	1¼ cups milk

Beat up eggs. Sift dry ingredients and add to eggs along with oil and half the milk. Mix well. Turn hominy grits into this. Mash with potato masher. Then beat with a spoon until well blended. Now add the rest of the milk and mix well. Turn into a greased baking dish, and bake at 375° until done (see note, p. 131), about 40 minutes.

Wheat

For many people in the world, wheat is the main source of protein. Although it does not supply a complete protein in itself, combined with beans it becomes a much better source of protein (see bean section, especially the introduction, p. 5). The combination must be at the same meal if not in the same dish, however, to get the benefit of the increased value in protein. When combined with milk, too, wheat is much more nutritious. Many of these recipes call for milk, but of course you can serve milk along with the biscuits or other wheat foods made merely with water and get the same effect. Whole-wheat is more nutritious than white. If you want to make bread with it, it will taste better if you use half white and half whole-wheat flour. Biscuits, pancakes and the like are delicious made this way.

Biscuits — General Directions

Biscuits are among the most important items in any cook's arsenal, but especially for those who don't have much money. They are food for the gods with margarine and honey on them, and people will sit down to a meal with nothing but homemade soup and hot biscuits and say, "Oh, boy!"

The only two things about biscuits that take any skill are rubbing the margarine into the flour and judging the right amount of milk (or water) to use. Rubbing margarine into flour is explained elsewhere (p. 130); as to the milk, start by adding less than the recipe calls for. Stir the dough enough to mix, and then with your hands try to gather up all the ingredients into one coherent ball. If you can't, add a *little* more milk, and try again. If the dough gets too wet (is sticky), on the other hand, sprinkle 2 or 3 table-spoons of flour around in the bowl, and roll the ball of dough around in it.

Roll out to desired thickness on a clean, floured surface: bread-board, kitchen table or counter. Put a little pile of flour about a foot away from the dough to keep the surface and the rolling pin floured. If the dough sticks, pick it up and flour the working sur-face again. Keep the rolling pin floured so it won't stick either. Cut biscuits with a biscuit cutter (a small can like a tomato-paste can may be used — punch a hole in the closed end — or you can cut square biscuits with a knife); put them on a cookie sheet or flat pan of any kind with sides not above ½ inch. Bake as directed.

Other uses for biscuit dough are pinwheels, turnovers, or as topping for meat pies. For pinwheels, see p. 76; turnovers are de-scribed on p. 77. For pies, roll out somewhat thinner than usual, perhaps ¼ inch, and cut into desired shapes, or just cover the pie with this. Either way, put on top of the filling and bake at 400° about 20 minutes. This is mainly used for a fairly wet, unthickened chicken or beef hash, which will already have been cooked. Twenty minutes will cook the dough on top.

My Biscuits

These are the biscuits I learned from my mother-in-law. When I asked how to make those wonderful biscuits she served, she said, "Oh, just reduce the milk and put in more shortening." After some experimenting, this is what I use (I think they are very superior to the ones coming up in the next recipe, which I call "ordinary" biscuits):

2¼ cups sifted flour (or 2 cups unsifted flour)
1 tablespoon baking powder
1 teaspoon salt

3 ounces margarine, or 1½ ounces margarine and 1½ ounces lard
scant ½ cup milk

Sift dry ingredients together. Rub in fat (see p. 130). Add milk as in general directions, and roll out about ⁵⁄₁₆ inch thick. Bake in a hot oven until delicately browned (about 10 to 12 minutes in 450° oven).

Ordinary Biscuits

2¼ cups sifted flour (or 2 cups unsifted flour)
1 tablespoon baking powder
1 teaspoon salt

2 ounces margarine, or 1 ounce margarine and 1 ounce lard
½ to ⅔ cup milk

Make as above, but roll out ½ inch thick. This makes tall showy biscuits, but they are not nearly as delicate or delicious as the previous ones in my opinion. Bake at 450° 10 to 14 minutes.

Biscuits on Top of the Stove

Biscuits may be cooked on an iron griddle or frying pan. Have pan a little less hot than for pancakes (p. 31). (Flour dropped on the pan will be brown in a few seconds.) Lightly grease the pan, and when hot enough put in the biscuits about an inch apart. They should be rolled about ¼ inch thick, thinner than oven-baked biscuits. Cook until browned on both sides. These are not quite as good as oven-baked biscuits, but there is really not a great deal of difference. They have an agreeable crispness on the outside.

Dumplings for Chicken and Dumplings
(Flat Dumplings)

The only trick to these is to roll them out very, very thin. They will swell while cooking. Roll thinner than ¹⁄₁₆ inch if you can.

2 cups sifted flour
2 teaspoons baking powder
1 teaspoon salt

⅓ cup margarine
½ cup milk, about

Sift dry ingredients together. Rub in the margarine (see p. 130). Add enough milk to make a soft dough, as for biscuits (see gen-

eral directions for biscuits above). Roll out very thin, and cut in
1½-inch squares, or rectangles of roughly the same size. Have your
broth boiling on high heat. Drop in dumplings two at a time —
keep the broth boiling — and when all are in, reduce heat to low
and cover. Boil for 12 minutes.

French Pancakes

These are very thin, unrisen pancakes, always rolled up with a
filling.

> 1 cup sifted flour   1 large or 2 small eggs
> ¼ teaspoon salt   1 teaspoon margarine for pan
> 1 cup water or milk

Add liquid to flour and salt very slowly, stirring gently. Beat up
egg(s) lightly in a separate bowl and add to batter, again very
slowly and stirring gently. (Instead, you may mix this quickly
and let the batter rest about 20 minutes.) Put batter through a
sieve. It should be about the consistency of fairly heavy cream.
Have a small frying pan, the size you want your pancakes to be,
fairly hot. Add just enough margarine to film the bottom of the
pan, and then put just enough batter in to barely cover the bottom
of the pan, tilting it in all directions to make the batter run to
the sides. Cook until browned a little underneath (about 1
minute) and then turn and cook on the other side. To use, fill
the pancakes (see below), roll them up into a cylinder (it is de-
lightfully easy to do this), and lay them side by side on a platter.
Cover them with a sprinkling of powdered sugar (if a sweet filling) or some sauce or gravy.

French Pancakes with Jam

This is often used in France as a snack for children when they get
home from school. Just spoon about 2 teaspoons of jam down the
middle of each pancake and turn the two sides over on it to make a
kind of cylinder. Dust with powdered sugar. A tablespoon of
granulated sugar may be added to the pancake batter if you are
going to use them this way.

French Pancakes with Meat
or Vegetable Fillings

Creamed vegetables are good rolled up in these. Save some of the cream sauce to dribble over the top and dust with paprika. Spinach is particularly good this way.

These are also good filled with meat in sauce, but the meat should be very tender, almost soft, and chopped fairly small, as the pancakes are delicate and are not good with chunky things in them.

Chopped chicken livers in a sauce made with chicken stock are a good example of the sort of thing I mean. Sauté finely chopped onion in margarine until soft. Add chicken livers and cook until just done, turning up the heat a bit, perhaps, to brown them. Remove livers from the pan and chop fairly small. Add 2 tablespoons flour and ¼ teaspoon salt to the pan, cook a few minutes, and add chicken stock (probably made by boiling the other giblets — see p. 93) to make the sauce (see p. 100). Fill each pancake with some of the livers and some of the sauce, lay them side by side on a platter (keeping them warm in the oven) and pour some sauce over all. (They should not swim in the sauce. Just dribble several tablespoonfuls over the top.)

Plain Muffins

2 cups sifted flour
1 tablespoon baking powder
½ teaspoon salt
3 tablespoons sugar

1 egg
¼ cup oil or melted fat
1 cup milk

Sift together dry ingredients. Add the rest of the ingredients and stir just enough to mix (the batter will be lumpy, but if you stir it a lot you will get little tunnels in the muffins and they will be rubbery). Spoon into greased muffin tins and bake about 20 minutes at 400°. This makes 12 muffins about 2 inches in diameter. Don't fill the cups quite full.

Plain Pancakes

2 cups flour
1 tablespoon baking powder
1 teaspoon salt
2 tablespoons sugar

2 eggs
2 tablespoons oil or melted fat
1½ cups milk

Sift together dry ingredients. Add other ingredients and mix with a wire whisk until well blended. Pour batter slowly onto hot, ungreased frying pan until rounds reach desired size. Frying pan should be hot enough for drops of water to dance around on it a few seconds before sizzling out. Get your fingers dripping and flick a few drops on to see. For electric frying pan, set at 380°. "Bake" until nicely browned on both sides, about 2 to 3 minutes in all. They are ready to turn over when they begin to bubble. Turn them only once.

Use more flour if you want a thicker pancake, less if you want them thinner.

Buttermilk Pancakes

2 cups flour
1 teaspoon salt
1 teaspoon soda
1 tablespoon sugar

2 tablespoons oil or melted fat
1 or 2 eggs, beaten
2 cups buttermilk (scant)

Mix and cook as for plain pancakes.

Panade with Celery (a Bread Soup)

4 or 5 large stalks celery, chopped
    fairly fine, about 2 cups
2 tablespoons margarine
4 tablespoons water
4 cups hot water

1 teaspoon salt
½ pound (about 8 slices) stale
    bread, broken up
1 egg
2 cups milk

Simmer celery in margarine and 4 tablespoons water, covered, until soft. Add 4 cups water, salt and bread, and simmer, covered, about 30 minutes, until bread is soft. Beat up soup with a whisk or egg beater until it is smooth. Beat egg in a separate bowl and add milk.

Add this to the soup. Reheat the soup slowly, but do not let it boil.

This is a delicious soup, good enough to serve even if you don't have any stale bread and have to use fresh. It makes a fairly substantial lunch all by itself.

Mixed Vegetable Panade

An excellent vegetable soup if you don't have any meat to put in it.

1 pound soup vegetables — carrots, onions, celery, turnips, parsnips, summer vegetables in season

3 tablespoons bacon grease or other fat

salt and pepper

1 tablespoon parsley

pinch of thyme leaves

1 cup canned tomatoes or equivalent (see p. 130)

3 cups water

2 slices leftover bread or toast

1 cup milk

Chop very fine or grate the vegetables and sauté them in the fat for a few minutes. Add salt and pepper, parsley and thyme, and let simmer in the fat about 10 minutes, covered. Now add tomatoes, juice and all, then add water and bread or toast. Simmer all together, covered, about 40 minutes. Now beat the soup with a wire whisk or spoon until the toast or bread is incorporated into the soup as a thickener. Then add the milk. Reheat slowly and taste for seasoning.

Spaghetti, Macaroni and Other Pastas

In the United States we tend to think of the various forms of pasta, or paste (flour and water, mainly), as a foundation on which fairly complicated dishes are built. In Italy, however, it is often eaten more or less for itself, very simply "dressed," perhaps only with oil or butter and garlic, or with only a few simple things added. For all but the well-heeled, it is often almost the whole meal. In this section, some of the simpler recipes are given. Pasta is not as cheap nowadays as some of the other starches, but it is still cheaper than a lot of other things, and it is mighty good.

In general, pasta should be cooked in a quantity of salted water for about 15 minutes before being drained and dressed. There are nearly always directions on the package, but if there are none, 3 quarts of water with one tablespoon of salt is usually right for a pound of pasta. Bring the water to a boil and add the pasta slowly enough so that it continues to boil without stopping. Boil uncovered for about 15 minutes, or until soft enough to eat but not entirely limp.

If you are going to put pasta in soup, however, see that it boils five minutes longer than called for on the package directions, or 20 minutes in all if there are none. It should be a little limp for soup, I think.

In general, one kind of pasta can be substituted for another, with just one caveat. If the pasta is to be simply dressed with something like oil and garlic or cheese and egg, use a solid kind of pasta like spaghetti or linguine, not a hollow kind like macaroni. Water is very difficult to drain out of the hollow kind, and makes a simple dressing mushy.

Macaroni Creole

½ pound macaroni	good pinch thyme leaves
2 tablespoons margarine	salt
1 tablespoon flour	whole onion stuck with a clove
1 stalk celery, chopped fine	1-pound can tomatoes
1 large onion, chopped fine	1 small green pepper
1 tablespoon parsley	salt and pepper

Make a roux (see p. 100) with margarine and flour. Add celery, onion, parsley and thyme. Let this simmer over medium heat, uncovered, a few minutes. Meanwhile add macaroni to boiling water with salt, onion and clove in it and cook according to general directions above. Drain. Now drain juice from canned tomatoes into the celery mixture, put on high heat and stir steadily until it thickens. Add tomatoes, broken into smallish pieces, and green pepper chopped fairly small. Season with salt and pepper, cook a few more minutes and taste for seasoning. Celery will still be a little crunchy. Add drained macaroni to sauce and serve.

Spaghetti with Eggs and Cheese

1 pound spaghetti, boiled (see directions)	¼ teaspoon salt
3 eggs	½ to 1 cup grated cheese

Drain spaghetti. Beat up the eggs and salt in a large mixing bowl. Add grated cheese. Add spaghetti and toss like a salad until all the egg and cheese are evenly distributed in the spaghetti. Put into a greased shallow baking dish, pat down and bake 20 minutes at 325°.

Spaghetti with Green Sauce

¾ pound spaghetti, boiled (see above)

2 ounces margarine

2 tablespoons basil

2 tablespoons parsley

8 ounces cream cheese, softened

⅓ cup Parmesan, or other yellow cheese, grated (optional)

¼ cup oil

1 clove garlic mashed to a cream

pepper

⅔ cup boiling water, or more

Drain spaghetti. To make sauce, mash margarine, basil and parsley together. Blend in all other ingredients but the water and mix well. Add boiling water gradually until you get the desired consistency. I like mine about like a thin cream sauce. Pour over spaghetti and serve.

Pasta with Oil, Garlic and Red Pepper

This is very sturdy stuff. My son says you should put on chapstick before eating it. I love it.

1 pound pasta without holes, boiled

3 large cloves garlic, mashed

½ to 1 hot red pepper

¼ cup oil

While pasta is boiling, pound together the garlic and red pepper until garlic becomes pink and pepper is broken up in small pieces. Brown this *slowly* in the oil in a large pot. Drain pasta very carefully, getting it as dry as possible. Now add pasta to oil and garlic and toss in pan until pasta is evenly coated. Larger pieces of pepper may be removed before tossing.

Spaghetti with Peas and Tomato Sauce

1 pound spaghetti, boiled (see directions)

3 to 4 tablespoons pork fat

2 medium onions, coarsely chopped

1½ 10-ounce cans tomato purée or equivalent (see p. 130)

½ pound green peas, or 10-ounce pkg., frozen

salt and pepper

Use bacon grease for this, or lard, or fat from salt pork. Oil may be substituted in part, but it won't be as good. Sauté onions in fat until soft. Add tomato purée and blend with onions and fat. You may want to thin the sauce with a little boiling water. Add peas, season with salt and pepper, and simmer uncovered very slowly for about 30 minutes. Serve over drained spaghetti. Serves 5 to 6. This is very good indeed.

Spaghetti with Tomato Sauce

This is very good served as an accompaniment to meat. With salad or a vegetable it makes a complete meal. Or it may be served as a separate course before the main course. It makes a good lunch with grated cheese served on top.

The tomato sauce may be made in various ways. I make mine just as for spaghetti sauce with ground beef (see p. 63), but substitute meat stock for the water, and omit the beef. If you wish to use canned tomatoes in the sauce, add flour to the onions and garlic sautéed in the oil or margarine, and cook a few minutes before adding the tomatoes, to thicken the sauce.

Eggs

Omelets

Omelets are not hard to cook; they are just hard to describe. Start with a 2- or 3-egg omelet, as it goes quicker. It really is best to keep a frying pan, with gently sloping sides and fairly heavy, just for omelets. Failing this, be sure your pan is perfectly clean. Rub some margarine all over the inside and then wipe almost all of it out. Have your pan on medium to medium-high heat a minute or two, then add about 1 tablespoon margarine. When it is melted, pour in 2 or 3 well-beaten eggs, seasoned with salt and pepper, and maybe some chervil (good pinch) and chives (1 to 2 teaspoons fresh, chopped). Let it sit there until the edges are set a little (20 seconds, maybe). Then gently with a fork lift up (don't push back) an edge of the egg mixture and let the runny part run under.

Do this all around the pan. Have a spatula handy and change to that as the egg gets more set. Tilt the pan toward the side where you are lifting the egg. Keep doing this all around the pan until most of the runny part has run under and set, leaving just a little runny egg on top. Toward the end, slide your spatula farther under the omelet so that it will be ready to turn over. When it is ready, turn half of it over on the other half (this is not tricky; just lift it and fold it like a sheet) and ease the omelet onto a hot serving dish or plate.

The whole thing takes about 3 minutes. After the first 20 seconds, it requires constant fussing but it goes very fast. You will get the hang of making omelets after a try or two. It is well worth knowing how, as you can come up with a delicious main dish in about 5 minutes.

A cheese omelet is simply made by sprinkling grated cheese over the egg during the first 20 seconds.

Omelets may be filled with a variety of things. One of my favorites is chicken livers. Sauté some sliced onions in margarine, and then add livers and sauté until lightly browned. Sprinkle with salt and pepper, chop into thumbnail-size pieces and put on omelet just before you turn it over. Turn omelet over on filling and slide out of pan to serve.

Bits of ham added to cream sauce seasoned with parsley may be used this way. You should have more ham than sauce.

Various sauces can be used to fill omelets, for example, Creole Sauce (p. 23) but use less liquid; you will want a much higher proportion of solid ingredients.

After cooking the omelet, wipe out the pan with a paper towel or a clean dry rag, and it will then be ready to use again.

Country Style Omelet *or Scramble*

I use 1 medium potato, cut into small dice, for each 2 eggs, but you may vary proportions. Sauté potatoes and diced onions in bacon grease or other fat until soft. Salt the potatoes, add beaten eggs, lightly seasoned, and scramble as for plain scrambled eggs. This is very good.

Crumb Omelet

3 eggs
½ cup toast crumbs, about (see
   p. 129)
½ cup boiling milk

½ teaspoon salt or less
pepper
1 to 2 tablespoons margarine

Wet the toast crumbs with the milk and set aside to cool. Beat up the eggs with the salt and pepper until they are fairly fluffy. Put a heavy frying pan on a medium-high burner to heat up. You need not use your omelet pan for this. Combine eggs and crumb mixture and mix until well blended. Melt the margarine in the hot pan and pour the omelet in. Reduce heat to medium. Let this set for 5 minutes or so. Then treat it like a regular omelet, lifting up the edges and tilting the pan so the runny part can run under and set. Cook until there is just a little runny part left on top. Fold over, put on a hot platter and serve. It should be nicely browned.

Soufflé Omelet

2 eggs, separated
1 tablespoon cornstarch
⅓ cup cold milk
pinch marjoram

scant ½ teaspoon salt
pepper
1 tablespoon margarine

Put cornstarch in a bowl. Add a little milk gradually, mixing to a smooth paste. Then add the rest of the milk and mix carefully. Now beat up egg yolks with the seasonings in a second bowl. Add the cornstarch mixture. Then beat up the egg whites in a third bowl with an extra pinch of salt until they are stiff and will hold a peak (see p. 129). Carefully fold them into the egg-yolk mixture.

Melt the margarine in a frying pan heated to medium high and pour the omelet into it. Reduce heat to medium and cover. Let it cook 6 to 8 minutes, or until the bottom is browned and you can fold it over. Check it occasionally as burners and pans vary. This should be cooked in a heavy pan with a well-fitting top, but it need not be one consecrated to omelets. After folding omelet over, ease it onto a heated platter and serve at once.

Scrambled Eggs and Corn

4 to 6 eggs
bacon, cut in 1-inch pieces
1 pound can cream-style corn,
   about

4 to 6 tablespoons milk
salt and pepper

Fry as much bacon as you want to use in this (ends and pieces are
fine and much cheaper) until brown. Pour off most of the grease
to use another time. Add the corn to the frying pan and heat. Beat
eggs and milk and seasonings together until well mixed. Pour into
the corn mixture in the frying pan and scramble together until set.
If you don't want to use any bacon, just scramble eggs and corn
together in a bit of margarine or bacon grease, 1 tablespoon or so.

Scrambled Eggs and Spinach

4 eggs
1 10-ounce pkg. frozen
   chopped spinach,
   cooked

2 tablespoons margarine
1 onion, chopped fine
salt and pepper

For cooking spinach, see note on p. 119. Sauté onion in margarine
until soft. Add spinach, mix well and sauté a few minutes more.
Beat up eggs with salt and pepper. Pour into pan with spinach
and scramble as usual. This is both delicious and easy.

Eggs with Tomatoes and Green Peppers

This is a delicious summer dish when the vegetables are in season.

4 eggs
1 green pepper
2 fresh tomatoes
1 onion, finely chopped

1 clove garlic, mashed
2 tablespoons oil
salt

Cut green pepper into thin strips. Peel the tomatoes (plunge each
one in boiling water for 1 minute for ease in peeling), discard the
seeds and cut into dice. Sauté onions, garlic and green pepper in
the oil until soft. Add the diced, fresh tomatoes. (This is one
time when fresh are very superior to canned. Save this dish for

the time when tomatoes and green peppers are cheap.) Cook un-covered over low heat until everything is soft and mushy. Break eggs in one at a time (they do not need to be beaten), stirring constantly. Season with salt. Raise heat to medium and stir rapidly until the mixture is nice and fluffy. Serve at once.

Egg and Cheese Fritters

3 eggs	2 teaspoons parsley
1 cup grated cheese (about 3 ounces)	1 teaspoon basil
	¼ teaspoon salt, or less
3 slices bread, grated to make soft crumbs	pepper
	oil for frying

Put the eggs in a mixing bowl and beat until light. Add all the rest of the ingredients but the oil, and mix well but lightly with a fork. Don't add too many crumbs; mixture should be fairly wet. Have oil, about ⅛ inch deep, almost smoking (about 400° to 420° in electric frying pan). Put mixture in pan by the tablespoonful and flatten cakes till about ¼ to ⅜ inch thick. Fry until brown on both sides, about 4 minutes in all.

Cheese

English Monkey

1 cup grated cheese	½ teaspoon salt
½ cup soft bread crumbs (see p. 129)	1 egg
	¼ teaspoon prepared mustard
1 cup hot milk	5 to 6 slices toast, spread with margarine
2 tablespoons margarine	

Soak crumbs in hot milk 10 to 20 minutes. Melt cheese and mar-garine over simmering water (in a double boiler, or a small sauce-pan in a large shallow pan with simmering water in it); it will probably take 3 or 4 minutes. Add crumbs and milk, and salt. Stir thoroughly. Beat up egg until light with mustard in a separate bowl. Add this to the cheese mixture, still over simmering water, and cook until thickened. Serve over toast spread with margarine.

(Old dry toast is best for this. Set in the oven to warm before using.)

Grits with Cheese

½ cup grits, (see p. 24), cooked, (makes about 2 cups)
2 ounces margarine
1 clove garlic, mashed

2 eggs, beaten
¼ teaspoon salt
⅓ cup milk
4 ounces cheese, grated

Cook grits, if possible, in a casserole or pot that can be put in the oven. While grits is cooking, melt margarine in a small frying pan or saucepan and add garlic. Let this cook slowly a few minutes over low heat and then remove garlic. Beat up the eggs and salt in a bowl and then add the milk. When grits is cooked, add the cheese and the melted margarine with garlic flavor and stir until the cheese is melted. Then add egg mixture and mix well. Bake at 350°, uncovered, for 30 minutes. This is very good and makes a satisfying main dish.

Macaroni and Cheese

6 ounces macaroni
2 to 3 quarts water
2 teaspoons salt, about
8 ounces cheese, grated
2 eggs
¼ teaspoon salt

¼ teaspoon prepared mustard (optional)
few drops Tabasco or Texas hot sauce (optional)
2 cups milk

Bring water to a boil in a large saucepan with 2 teaspoons salt. Add macaroni slowly so that water does not stop boiling. Boil hard for 10 minutes and drain (or follow package directions, but do not boil the full time as it will cook more in the oven). Run cold water over the macaroni. Meanwhile grate the cheese.

Beat up eggs in a mixing bowl together with the ¼ teaspoon salt. If your cheese has too bland a flavor, the addition of mustard and hot sauce to the eggs makes a tastier dish. Add 2 cups milk to the egg mixture and mix thoroughly. Put one third of the macaroni in the bottom of a greased oven dish and then one third of the cheese. Add a second and third layer of macaroni and cheese, alternately. Pour milk and egg mixture over this. It should come up nearly to the top. If it doesn't, add more milk and tilt pan all around to mix. Bake at 350° until set and somewhat browned, about 45 minutes or more depending on depth of dish.

Cheese Pudding

2 cups grated cheese, about 7 ounces
4 slices bread, spread with margarine and cut into cubes
3 eggs, beaten
¼ teaspoon salt

few drops Texas hot sauce (optional)
¼ teaspoon prepared mustard (optional)
2 cups milk

This will have a better flavor with hot sauce and mustard added to the eggs if the cheese is bland. Lay bread cubes spread with margarine in the bottom of a casserole. Beat eggs and seasoning and add milk. Pour egg and milk mixture over the bread cubes. Let rest for 1 hour for bread to absorb liquid. Add grated cheese, stir up and bake until set, about 30 minutes, in a 375° oven.

Cheese Rice

A very simple dish of hot boiled rice with grated cheese added, and tossed lightly with a fork until cheese is melted, is very good. A more delicious dish may be made as follows:

1 cup or more boiled rice
1 cup tomato sauce or purée or canned tomatoes thickened with a roux (see p. 100)
2 eggs, beaten

½ teaspoon salt
pepper
1 cup (about 3 ounces) grated cheese

Mix all these ingredients well and bake until egg is set (about 30 minutes in a 375-to-400° oven). One and one-half cups cream sauce (p. 102) may be substituted for the tomatoes.

Welsh Rarebit

1 to 1½ cups (3 to 5 ounces) grated cheese
2 tablespoons margarine
1 teaspoon Worcestershire sauce
½ teaspoon salt

½ teaspoon paprika
½ to 1 teaspoon prepared mustard
1 cup milk
2 eggs

Melt margarine in a frying pan. Add seasonings and grated cheese. Stir over medium heat until cheese is soft. Add milk and then lightly beaten eggs. Stir until thick, about 5 minutes. Serve on toast.

****

II

Soup

****

Soup is one of the greatest boons to the cook with a small budget. Fortunately it is also a great boon to anyone who likes good food, for there is nothing any better than good soup, and there are many delicious kinds. I have included about 30 recipes, and none of them is expensive.

Besides tasting good, there are several other good things about soup. With care, a little goes a long way. I say "with care" because you cannot put two or three things in some water and have a tasty soup. With the exception of some of the bean soups, very little soup is really good on the basis of just water unless it includes some kind of meat or bones, or both, or has a lot of milk added to it. However, if you are careful to save and boil up all your bones, except for pork bones (which are not much good for anything that I know of), you will have the beginning of some excellent soup. For example, even if you have boiled a chicken and used both chicken and broth, perhaps for chicken and dumplings, you can take the same bones, skin and anything left from the chicken, boil it all 2 more hours and you will have a second stock (see p. 103) that will do perfectly well in lots of soups. Any leftover gravy is also good for the soup pot. Furthermore, you can often get bones at the grocery store for very little money. Add some flavoring vegetables like onions to these and you can make a very good base for soup.

Next, soup is good for using up odds and ends. Again care is needed to have flavors that go well together. Using up leftovers to make delicious dishes is a true test of a good cook. By hoarding your resources carefully, by becoming familiar with standard recipes, and by "taking thought," you can be proud of your soups-out-of-nothing and can be sure of getting enthusiastic response from the people you cook for.

Hoarding your resources carefully means buying the cheapest-per-ounce can of tomato, for example, using what is needed for the day and putting up the rest in a clean glass jar in the refrigerator to be added to soups, stews and the like as required. Many recipes call for a little of this or that — just half a cup of tomato may make the difference between usable and delicious soup. Most vegetables will keep a fairly long time in the refrigerator until needed. If you make soup a lot you will soon get good at surveying the bits you have and making a good soup out of them.

It is helpful to read recipes and to see what will make a good combination in a soup. Reading the recipe for chili con carne, for example, or for keema, may give you some good ideas about how to use leftover ground beef in a soup.

By "taking thought," I mean the kind of planning that could have you deliberately serving a vegetable one evening, say, which you want to have some of in the soup the next day. In that case, save back the amount needed for the next day rather than putting it on the table to tempt your eaters. If the vegetable the first day is a bit skimpy, add some fried bread cubes, or a bit of boiled pasta and a little extra seasoning to stretch it out.

Another advantage to soup is that even with a fairly light soup you can take the edge off a hefty appetite before it attacks the more expensive part of the meal. If you are going to have chicken salad for Sunday dinner, as I often do, make an egg and lemon soup out of the broth from boiling the chicken, and serve it first. Even sneakier, serve small bowls of lentil or split pea soup before the Sunday joint.

Finally, many of the sturdy soups can make almost the whole meal. Add hot biscuits or hoecakes and a substantial dessert made with eggs, like a rice pudding. Or maybe just make a substantial bread like cornmeal muffins. Make a lot and pass molasses with them for the sweet. Corn bread and molasses may not sound like much but it is a much-loved staple where I live. Hot corn bread or muffins or hoecake with margarine melted on it and molasses on top is really something.

Other bean soup recipes found in this book:

Baked Bean Soup, p. 7.
Bean Soup (Greek Fassoulada), p. 9.
Portuguese Red Bean Soup, p. 11.

Carrot Soup

4 medium carrots, sliced thin	1¼ cups boiled rice, or 2 medium
1 onion, coarsely chopped	potatoes, sliced (better with
salt and pepper	potatoes, I think)
4 cups well-flavored chicken broth	1 cup milk
2 to 3 tablespoons margarine	

Simmer carrots, onions and salt and pepper, covered, in margarine about 15 minutes, stirring occasionally. Add chicken broth and rice or potatoes to the vegetables, and simmer, covered, about 40 minutes more. Put the soup through a sieve, return to the pot, add milk, reheat slowly and serve. Most recipes call for rice, saying you can substitute potatoes. I think it has a much pleasanter consistency with the potatoes, and it is much easier to sieve.

Chicken Chowder

See recipe p. 90.

Chicken Giblet Soup

2 sets chicken giblets	salt and pepper
1 small onion, chopped fine	pinch of mace
1 small carrot, chopped fine	1 small turnip, sliced thin
1 to 2 tablespoons margarine	another tablespoon margarine
3 cups water	1 tablespoon flour

Sauté onion and carrot in margarine for a few minutes, then sprinkle with salt, cover and let them "sweat" a few minutes until soft. Add cold water, chicken necks, gizzards, hearts and wing tips, if you have remembered to cut them off, and salt and pepper and mace. Reserve livers for later. Bring all this to a boil very slowly on medium heat, and then simmer, covered, 2 to 2½ hours. Add the turnip slices and simmer 10 minutes longer, or until they are transparent. In the meantime sauté the livers in the extra tablespoon of margarine, gently at first, and then turn up the heat to brown them, just a few minutes in all. Remove livers, reduce heat, add the flour and brown slowly in the same pan. Ladle a little of the soup into it and stir until it thickens. Return this sauce to the soup. Now put the livers through a fairly fine sieve. Next remove the necks and wing tips, if any, from the soup and discard. Then put the rest of the soup through the sieve. If the gizzards and hearts won't go through, I just throw them away. Put the sieved liver and soup back in the pan and reheat. Taste for seasoning and serve.

This is very good and surprisingly hearty. It is not as much trouble as it sounds.

Corn Chowder

10-ounce pkg. frozen corn or 1½ to 2 cups fresh
⅓ cup salt pork, diced (about 2 ounces)
1 medium onion, coarsely chopped
3 medium potatoes, diced
2 cups hot water
salt and pepper
3 cups milk
8 to 12 soda crackers (2 x 2 inches, about)

Try out pork in the bottom of a soup pot. Pour off excess fat and sauté onions in the remaining fat. When onion is soft, add potatoes and hot water and simmer, covered, 25 to 30 minutes. Add corn and cook 2 to 3 minutes. Add salt carefully, as the pork is salty and so are the crackers to be put in. Add pepper liberally. Then add milk and heat gradually for flavors to blend. Do not boil. Just before serving, add soda crackers.

Egg Chowder

4 eggs
3 to 4 ounces salt pork, diced (about ½ cup)
2 to 4 potatoes, diced small
1 medium onion, coarsely chopped
4 cups milk
salt and pepper

Try out salt pork and pour off excess fat. Add potatoes and onion and sauté until soft. Add warmed milk and heat very slowly for flavors to blend. When just below boiling (it begins to puff a little) add salt and pepper and whole eggs, one at a time. Cook uncovered on low heat, keeping the soup below the boiling point, 5 to 10 minutes, depending on how hard you like your eggs. Dish each egg into a soup bowl and pour soup over it. This is very good, and with a vegetable or fruit makes just about a whole meal.

Egg and Lemon Soup

This is delicious made with either chicken stock or fish stock. It is better if the stock is strongly flavored. Second stock may be used but in that case you probably should add a chicken bouillon cube or two.

2 eggs	salt and pepper
juice of a lemon	thickener (see directions)
4 cups stock	

Make a roux with 2 tablespoons margarine and two of flour. Add stock gradually as for sauce (p. 100). Simmer a few minutes until thickened. Beat up the eggs in a bowl and add the lemon juice to them. Incorporate this (p. 101) into the soup. Reheat and serve, but do not let it boil after adding the egg mixture.

I think this soup, which is one of my very favorites, is best thickened with the roux. But you may omit the roux and add ¼ cup rice, or any pasta suitable for soup.

Fish Chowder

1 pound fish fillets or equivalent amount of whole fish, dressed	4 medium potatoes, diced
2 tablespoons margarine	4 cups milk
1 onion, coarsely chopped	1 tablespoon salt
2 cups water	1 teaspoon black pepper

In a large soup pot, sauté onion in margarine until soft. Add 2 cups water and bring to a boil. Add potatoes and fish. Simmer without seasoning, covered, for 30 minutes. Add milk, salt and pepper, and reheat slowly to blend flavors.

This may be made with salt pork instead of margarine, and I think it is better to do so when your fish is strongly flavored. Proceed as with corn chowder (see p. 45) until onions are sautéed.

Caribbean Chowder

1 pound fish fillets, or equivalent amount of whole fish, dressed
2 cups water
4 medium potatoes, diced
1 large onion, sliced
1 28-ounce can tomatoes
2 teaspoons salt
2 to 4 cups chicken stock (may be second stock or made with bouillon cubes)

1 teaspoon seafood seasoning
2 to 4 tablespoons sherry (optional)
1 tablespoon margarine
juice of 1 lemon

Put the first 8 ingredients in a soup pot and bring to a boil. Simmer, covered, for 30 minutes. Five minutes before serving, add the sherry, if used, and the margarine. Just before serving add the lemon juice. This, with bread, makes the whole meal for four hungry people. It is delicious without the sherry, though that is a pleasant addition.

Fish Purée

This is a good way to use a not very good tasting fish or one that has unpleasant skin. Even croaker makes a good soup this way.

1 pound fish fillets, or equivalent amount of whole fish dressed and with bones removed after initial cooking
4 cups water
1 stalk celery cut into 1-inch pieces

1 carrot, quartered
1 onion, quartered
1 parsnip, if available
2 bay leaves
salt and pepper
1 tablespoon lemon juice

Bring to a boil the water, celery, carrot, onion, parsnip, if used, bay leaves, salt and pepper. Simmer, covered, at least 20 minutes. Add fish or fillets and simmer again, covered, until fish is quite tender (about 15 minutes for fillets, more for whole fish). Drain the soup, reserving the liquid. Remove the bones and skin from the fish if whole. Sieve the solid ingredients or mash them to a pulp. Put back in the liquid, reheat and taste for seasoning.

Ham and Bean Soup

This is an excellent way to use a ham bone and a little or a lot of ham. Ham and beans are naturals together, and with the addition of some seasonings (whatever you like) and one or more of the usual soup vegetables, such as onions, carrots and celery, you have a fine soup.

You may use canned or dried beans. If you use canned beans, rinse them thoroughly or your soup will taste canned. Boil the ham bone in water to cover for at least 2 hours. Strain the soup stock and add the beans, seasonings and soup vegetables to it. Cut up any ham pieces stuck to the bone and add. Cook everything together until blended and the vegetables are done.

Dried beans are cheaper and they can be simmered right in with the ham bone, though this means that whatever debris comes off the ham bone will remain in the soup. If the fuel is not too much of a problem, cook the beans (see p. 6) and the ham bone separately, and then proceed as with the canned beans.

Ham and Bean Soup with Potatoes

8 to 16 ounces ham
1 pound beans (Great Northern are best for this, I think)
2½ quarts water
salt to taste
3 to 4 medium potatoes, cut into chunks

2 large onions, coarsely chopped
2 cloves garlic, mashed
2 tablespoons lard or other fat
2 tablespoons parsley
1½ teaspoons paprika

Soak beans overnight in the water. Next day put beans and the same water on to boil with the ham cut into six chunks (or one for each person you want to serve). When boiling reduce heat and simmer, covered, 1¾ hours. Taste for salt. Meanwhile sauté potatoes, onions, and garlic in fat until they are browned a bit (some kind of pork fat is best for this). Then add to the soup. Add parsley and paprika, and more salt for the potatoes. Simmer 15 minutes more, or until potatoes are thoroughly done.

Lentil Soup

See recipe in "Hard Times," p. 10.

Mint Soup

This is an unusual combination of flavors but it is delicious even when made with bouillon cubes. Since mint will grow like a weed, even in the house, this is very inexpensive indeed.

4 or 5 large mint leaves, or ⅛ teaspoon dried mint
1 large onion, coarsely chopped
2 tablespoons margarine
2 cloves garlic
5 coriander seeds

¾-inch piece red pepper, or ⅛ teaspoon dried red pepper, or ¼ teaspoon hot sauce
salt
4 cups stock (may be made with chicken bouillon cubes)

Sauté onion in margarine in a soup pot until soft. Meanwhile mash garlic, coriander seeds, red pepper (unless you are using hot sauce) and a pinch or two of salt together. Add to the onion and margarine. Add stock and simmer a few minutes. Chop up mint leaves and add, or add dried mint. Add hot sauce, if used. Simmer about 5 minutes more.

Onion Soup with Milk and Eggs

4 medium onions, sliced thin and halved
2 tablespoons margarine
1½ cups milk
3 cups water
pepper, white if you have it

good pinch mace
2 teaspoons cornstarch
¾ cup more of milk
3 eggs
salt

Lightly brown onions in margarine in a soup pot. Add 1½ cups milk, water, pepper and mace, and simmer slowly, covered, about an hour. Meanwhile mix cornstarch carefully with ¾ cup milk, adding a little milk at a time until it is very smooth. Add this to the soup and cook a few minutes more. Remove soup from heat. Beat up eggs until light. Incorporate (see p. 101) into the soup, making sure the soup has been off the heat a minute or two before you do this, as it will boil more easily after the egg is added. (The soup will curdle if the eggs boil. You can eat it — it really tastes quite all right, but it looks horrible.) This is a very nourishing version of onion soup and is delicious.

Panade with Celery

See recipe in "Hard Times," p. 31.

Mixed Vegetable Panade

See recipe in "Hard Times," p. 32.

Split Pea Soup with Ham Bone

1 pound dried split peas	⅛ teaspoon thyme leaves
1 medium onion, sliced	pepper
1 to 2 carrots, quartered	salt to taste, at end
bunch of celery leaves	3 quarts water (some stock or
1 large bay leaf	milk may be substituted for
ham bone	part of the water — milk would
1 tablespoon parsley	not be added until the end)

Put all ingredients but salt and milk, if used, in a soup pot and bring to a boil. Simmer, covered, about 2 hours. Take out bone and put the rest of the soup through a sieve. Bits of ham may be returned to the soup if desired. This is better if some second chicken stock (p. 103) is substituted for some of the water. No milk is needed if that is used. Otherwise 2 cups of milk may be added at the end. Add salt to taste.

Another Split Pea Soup

See "Hard Times," p. 12.

Pistou

This is a wonderful summer soup and it requires no stock. Snap beans, potatoes, tomatoes and onions are the basic vegetables for it. Other summer vegetables may be added as desired.

1 10-ounce pkg. frozen snap beans, or ½ pound fresh
1 large potato, diced
2 tomatoes, peeled and diced, or 1-pound can, pieces broken up
1 onion, coarsely chopped
1 green pepper, diced (optional)
1 yellow squash or zucchini (optional)
3 to 4 cups water

2 large cloves garlic
2 teaspoons dried basil
1 to 2 tablespoons olive oil or other vegetable oil
salt
pepper, preferably red (1-inch piece)
2 ounces vermicelli or other fine pasta (two handfuls)

Add vegetables, salt and pepper to water boiling in a soup pot. Simmer, covered, about 20 minutes. Put garlic and basil in a mortar with 1 teaspoon of the oil and pound it. When thoroughly mashed, add the rest of the oil a bit at a time. After simmering the vegetables 20 minutes, add pasta and cook until soft (add 5 minutes to the package directions). Then ladle some soup into the mortar with the garlic mixture, and pour this combination back into the soup. Mix well, let stand a few minutes and serve.

Potato Soup

This is delicious made with onion, even better if you can find some leeks.

3 onions, quartered, or 1 onion and 4 leeks
2 tablespoons margarine
4 medium potatoes, sliced

2 cups water
1 teaspoon salt
4 cups milk
1 egg (optional)

Sauté onions, and leeks, if used, in margarine in a soup pot until soft. Add potatoes, salt and water and simmer, covered, until very soft, about 40 minutes. Put through a sieve, return to the pot, add milk and reheat slowly. An egg may be beaten up and incorporated (see p. 101) into the soup. Do not let it boil after adding the egg.

The classic recipes I've seen do not call for pepper, but I always add it to the onions and margarine. It smells so good.

Shepherd's Soup

½ cup salt pork, diced
2 onions, finely chopped
1 carrot, thinly sliced
1 to 1½ quarts water (or, better, stock)

3 potatoes, diced small
1 turnip, diced
salt and pepper

Try out salt pork in a soup pot. Reduce heat, add onions and carrot and cook gently, covered, for 10 minutes or so. Add water or stock and potatoes and simmer about 30 minutes more. Add turnip and salt and pepper to taste. Simmer again about 10 minutes longer or until turnip is transparent and potatoes are soft. Serve with toasted bread.

Spanish Soup

2 slices bacon, or ends and pieces, cut in 1-inch squares
2 large onions, coarsely chopped
1 stalk celery, chopped
1-pound can tomatoes
2 potatoes, diced
1½ to 2 quarts stock (may be made with bouillon cubes)

1 tablespoon vinegar
⅛ teaspoon thyme leaves
1 tablespoon parsley
nutmeg to taste
1 egg

Sauté the bacon in a soup pot until brown. Add onions and sauté until soft. Add celery and tomatoes and cook slowly a few minutes. Then add the rest of the ingredients except the egg. Simmer, covered, about 30 minutes. Incorporate the egg (see p. 101), reheat and serve. Do not let soup boil after adding the egg.

Turnip Soup

3 medium turnips, sliced and
quartered
1 onion, sliced and quartered
2 tablespoons margarine
2 cups stock
salt and pepper
2 teaspoons parsley and pinch of
thyme if stock is not well
seasoned

¼ teaspoon nutmeg
1 tablespoon margarine
1½ tablespoons flour
½ cup milk

Sauté onions and margarine in a soup pot until soft. Add stock, turnips, salt and pepper, nutmeg (and parsley and thyme if used). Simmer, covered, until turnips are almost done. This depends on the age of the turnips. Fresh young turnips take a very few minutes, say 5 to 10. Older ones, 5 to 10 minutes longer. They should become almost transparent. Then add manié "butter" (see p. 101), made from margarine and flour, and stir until thickened. Finally add milk and reheat, but do not boil. Serve at once. If turnips are not overcooked they have a delightful flavor. Overcooking makes them harsh and indigestible.

Turnip and Potato Soup

4 turnips, sliced thin
4 medium potatoes, sliced thin
4 to 5 cups water
1½ teaspoons salt

2 tablespoons margarine
2 to 3 cups milk
pepper

Simmer potatoes, water, salt and margarine, covered, about 30 minutes. Add turnips and simmer again, covered, until the turnips are just tender (see Turnip Soup for time). Put the soup through a sieve. Return it to the pot and add milk and pepper to taste. Reheat slowly but do not boil.

****

III

Fish

****

FISH IS ONE of the things that are relatively cheap even now, if you buy with caution, which generally means looking for the fish (fresh or frozen) that are plentiful in your area. (It used to be very cheap, and perhaps it will· be again some day.) It is also very quick to cook, is a splendid source of the best protein and it has little or no fat. It is ideal if you are overweight, or watching cholesterol or your blood pressure. It is also very good to eat.

Most fish recipes may be used for any kind of fish, and fresh or frozen fish may be cooked the same way as well. Fresh fish is marvelous if you live on the coast or are a fisherman yourself, but I find frozen very satisfactory. In general you will want to use a recipe which is fairly highly flavored if your fish is strongly flavored. A delicately flavored fish may be very simply cooked, like Plain Sautéed Fish (p. 58).

Cheap canned fish may be made into really excellent dishes too. There are three recipes in this chapter for sauces for them. The cheapest canned fish in my area are sardines, herring and mackerel. All three are delicious in any of these sauces, and can be served on toast, or over spaghetti or polenta, or rolled up in French pancakes.

These sauce recipes may also be used to make a very good Kedgeree out of cheap canned fish. For four to six people, or even more, sauté some onions in margarine, add rice as for pilaff (see p. 14), add canned fish and the liquid from the can combined with enough water for the rice, and then all the rest of the ingredients of the sauce except the thickener (flour or cornstarch), increasing them as needed, depending on how much rice you use. At the beach last summer I made one 1-pound can of mackerel feed nine people — using lots of rice! It made a very successful lunch.

Baked Fish Ginny

1 pound fish fillets (whole fish may be used)	juice of 1 lemon, or 1 tablespoon vinegar
2 ounces margarine	1 tablespoon parsley
2 large onions, coarsely chopped	salt and pepper

Put half the margarine, cut in thin pats, in the bottom of a shallow baking pan. Add half the onion, sprinkling it over the bottom of the pan. Lay fish fillets over this. Moisten with lemon or vinegar. Sprinkle with salt, pepper and parsley. Put small pieces of the rest of the margarine on top with the rest of the chopped onion. You may put mashed-potato cakes around it if you like, or parboiled potatoes, cut in quarters. Bake in moderate oven (350°) until it flakes easily, about 45 minutes.

The liquid which cooks out in the pan is delicious. You may make a fine sauce with it if you wish — though this is very good plain and needs no gilding — by incorporating an egg (see p. 101) into the liquid in the pan and cooking it over very low heat (do not let it boil) until it thickens. If the liquid has about cooked away, add ½ cup or so of boiling water and scrape up everything stuck to the bottom of the pan, and make a sauce with this. If you wish to make this sauce, omit the parsley in cooking the fish.

Another good sauce for this, especially if the fish has a strong flavor like perch, is Piquant Fish Sauce (p. 59).

Baked Fish Espagnole

1 pound fish fillets	2 tablespoons flour
bacon grease or oil	1 tablespoon parsley
salt and pepper	1 tablespoon lemon juice
½ teaspoon mushroom powder	2 tablespoons tomato purée or substitute (see p. 130)
2 to 3 slices bacon (ends and pieces are fine)	¼ cup water
2 tablespoons margarine	

Rub shallow baking dish with bacon grease or oil. Lay fish fillets in it. Season with salt and pepper and mushroom powder. Top with bacon. Dot with manié "butter" (see p. 101) made with the margarine and flour. Sprinkle with parsley. Mix lemon juice with tomato purée and water. Pour over fish. Bake at 375° for 30 to 40 minutes, or until fish flakes easily.

Baked Fish with Cream Sauce

1 pound fish fillets	1 tablespoon parsley
4 tablespoons margarine	salt and pepper
4 tablespoons flour	1 egg
2 cups milk	toast crumbs (see p. 129)
¼ teaspoon nutmeg	more margarine
grated rind of ½ lemon	

Make a roux (see p. 100) with margarine and flour. Make a sauce (see p. 100) with the milk. Add nutmeg, grated lemon rind, parsley, salt and pepper. Incorporate the egg (see p. 101). Put half the fish, salted, in a greased baking dish, then half the sauce. Repeat. Top with toast crumbs and dot with margarine. Bake in 350° oven for 1 hour.

Fish Chowder

See "Soup," p. 46.

Fish Purée

See "Soup," p. 47.

Fried Fish

For a pound of fish fillets mix a cup of cornmeal with ½ cup flour. Salt each piece of fish lightly on both sides. I generally use frozen fish fillets, thawed, but if the fish is fresh, and dressed, dip in water first and then add salt. Next, coat with cornmeal mixture and put in a pan of hot fat (about 380°, or about the temperature for pancakes), about ¼ inch deep. I like to use bacon grease if I have it; you may combine it with oil. If it browns too fast, reduce the heat — the fat should not smoke. Fry on both sides until brown and fish flakes easily, about 5 or 6 minutes in all for thin fillets, more for thicker fish. Serve immediately. Fish will get soggy if kept hot in the oven.

Kedgeree, or Fish with Rice

This is good with leftover fish, or fish poached in court bouillon (see p. 58) just for this purpose. Use any broth left (however it is seasoned) as all or part of the liquid. If you don't have any broth, chicken stock — even that made with chicken bouillon cubes — will do. See pp. 59–60 for ways to use cheap canned fish for this. This recipe may also be used for salmon or tuna fish in an emergency.

1 to 2 cups cooked fish or good canned fish	2½ cups liquid (see above)
2 tablespoons margarine	1 cup raw long-grain rice
2 onions, coarsely chopped	salt and pepper

Sauté onions in margarine. Add rice as for pilaff (p. 14). Add the rest of the ingredients and simmer until rice is done, about 30 minutes.

Caribbean Chowder

See Soup, p. 47.

Fish Poached with Tomatoes

1 pound fish fillets	1-pound can tomatoes
3 tablespoons margarine	1 tablespoon parsley
2 onions, coarsely chopped	juice ½ lemon (optional)
1 clove garlic, mashed	1 teaspoon salt
¼ teaspoon thyme leaves	pepper
½ bay leaf	1 tablespoon flour

Put 2 tablespoons of the margarine, onions, garlic, thyme and bay leaf in the bottom of a flame-proof casserole or pan. Add half the tomatoes from the can, breaking them up. Lay fillets on top and season with salt and pepper. Cover with remaining tomatoes, broken up, the juice from the can and the parsley. Add lemon juice if you wish; it is good with or without. Simmer slowly, covered, about 15 minutes. Remove fish to a platter and keep warm. Now cook liquid, uncovered, down to half its original quantity and add manié "butter" (see p. 101), made with the other tablespoon of margarine and 1 tablespoon flour. Stir until thickened. Pour over fish, and serve.

Plain Sautéed Fish

For any kind of fish that has a good flavor, this is one of the very best ways to cook it, I think. Put a combination of oil and margarine in a pan and melt margarine on low heat. Tilt pan several times to mix. You may then sauté some onion in this until almost soft before adding the fish, but if the fish is really *good*, like bluefish, omit the onion. Lay the fish in the margarine and oil and salt lightly. Sauté very gently until fish almost loses its transparency — just a very few minutes. Turn the fish over, salt it again lightly and sauté it until it is opaque and flakes easily, again only a few minutes. It should sauté *very* gently and cook until *just* done. If the fish is good, this is perfectly delicious.

If you want to cook a strongly flavored fish this way because you are in a hurry, sauté garlic in with the onion. When fish is done, remove from pan and make a tomato sauce for it, or one of the sauces (see pp. 59–60) right in the pan.

Court Bouillon and Sauces for Fish

Court Bouillon and Poaching Fish

1 to 3 cups water	small bay leaf
1 onion, sliced	2 tablespoons vinegar
1 small-to-medium carrot, sliced	½ teaspoon salt
2 teaspoons parsley	pepper
scant ⅛ teaspoon thyme leaves	

Put all this in a pan and bring to a boil. Simmer, covered, 30 minutes. Or, if you are ready to poach your fish, simmer 20 minutes before adding the fish, for flavors to blend.

Poaching time for fish varies according to thickness of fish or fillets, but it is very short. Five to ten minutes should do it for fillets. Up to 20 minutes perhaps for a whole fish. The flesh will become opaque and flake easily.

You will find poaching fish this way very useful if you only want to use half or part of a frozen fish package at the time when the fish is thawed. Then you can cook the first part any way you like and poach the rest. When it is done, drain it and refrigerate both fish and fish stock. The fish can be creamed (using half milk and half fish stock) to serve on toast or with noodles, rice, and so forth. (Flavor cream sauce with oregano, garlic and lemon juice — very good.) Or it may be made into a good salad (one recipe given below) and the fish stock saved for soup, especially Egg and Lemon Soup.

Piquant Fish Sauce (for Baked Fish Ginny, or other simply baked fish)

Remove fish from flame-proof baking dish and keep hot. There should be about a ½ cup of liquid in the bottom for a pound of fish fillets. If not, add enough boiled water to bring it up to that. Add to this 2 tablespoons tomato ketchup, 1 tablespoon Worcestershire sauce, 1 teaspoon curry powder and several drops of Tabasco or hot sauce. Bring all this to a boil and scrape edges to loosen everything stuck to the pan. (Do this off the stove if baking dish is not flame-proof and put the contents in a saucepan.) Simmer a few minutes to blend. Taste for flavor. Additions are to taste; add more of any of the flavorings as you like. Serve sauce separately from the fish.

Sauces for Cheap Canned Fish
(pound cans of herring, mackerel or sardines)

See pages 55–58 for various ways these sauces can be used. If fish is to be heated in a sauce, heat it slowly for flavors to blend.

Chinese Fish Sauce

2 tablespoons margarine	2½ tablespoons soy sauce
1 tablespoon cornstarch	½ teaspoon ground ginger
½ cup water, combined with ½ cup liquid from a can of fish	[no salt needed]

Melt margarine over low heat. Remove pan from heat and stir in cornstarch, with a wire whisk if you have one. With the pan still off the heat, stir in the cup of cold liquid slowly and carefully, blending as you add it. (If you have no liquid from a can, you may use stock made with a chicken bouillon cube — just be sure the liquid is cold when you add it.) Return pan to heat and keep stirring until sauce thickens and begins to boil. Add soy sauce and ginger. Cook 1 minute after it thickens and becomes somewhat transparent. Heat canned fish slowly in sauce.

These proportions are for very strongly flavored fish. You may wish to reduce soy sauce and ginger for a lighter flavored fish.

Curry Sauce for Fish

1 large onion, sliced
1 clove garlic, mashed
2 tablespoons margarine
1 tablespoon parsley
2 teaspoons curry powder, or to taste

2 tablespoons flour
1 cup liquid, including liquid from a can of fish

Sauté onions and garlic in margarine until soft. Add parsley and curry powder and sauté a minute or two more. Add flour to make a roux (see p. 100), and then liquid to make a sauce (see p. 100). Cook a few minutes more until flavors are blended.

Another Piquant Sauce

2 large cloves garlic, mashed
2 tablespoons margarine
3 tablespoons tomato ketchup

liquid from a can of fish
1 tablespoon parsley
good pinch ground cloves

Sauté garlic in margarine a few minutes. Add ketchup, juice from the can, parsley and ground cloves. Let this simmer a few minutes for flavors to blend. This is particularly good with canned mackerel, I think.

****

IV

"Make a Little Go a Long Way"

****

I USED TO BE irritated by this suggestion, from my mother or my mother-in-law, or whoever. I thought — you get the same amount of meat whether you've stretched it or not. Why bother? And not only that. One of the dreariest phrases in cookery is "meat stretcher." It sounds both mean and unappetizing and it often comes to just that. But I was forgetting about what makes a satisfying meal.

Suppose your budget for the week allows you to buy one pound of fish, one pound of ground beef and one chicken — that's all the meat you will have. If you fry up the whole pound of fish in one day, plain rice the next day isn't going to make much of a meal. But if you use half the fish for a chowder today and poach the rest, the next day you can make a fine rice and fish dish with what you've poached, and make some soup with the liquid you poached it in, like the delicious Egg and Lemon Soup, for lunch. This way you have a satisfying dinner both days. If the dinner has been good, few people will count up the ounces of fish or meat they have had.

So that's Monday and Tuesday of our hypothetical week. Wednesday you had better have a macaroni and cheese casserole, or polenta with cheese and tomato sauce. Thursday you'll be ready for some ground beef. Make it into spaghetti sauce, for example. Cook a pound of spaghetti, but save a third of the sauce for the next day. Next day make some pinwheels, making lots of biscuit dough, with maybe a little extra tomato to spoon over the top. Or you could use half the ground beef on Thursday for chili con carne with beans over rice or with pasta, and Friday the rest will go nicely in meat turnovers, or a rice casserole, or a macaroni casserole. If you have a freezer, or a good-sized freezing compartment, you can freeze the leftover ground beef and serve the two meals farther apart.

Now all you have to get through is Saturday before you have a bang-up dinner Sunday with the chicken. Give your people some lentils and rice, and make them a nice pie for dessert.

So we have had a lot of meat stretchers, but when you come to think of it, many of the best recipes in the world are really neither more nor less than meat stretchers. Meat pies, shepherd's pie, filled French pancakes, liver fritters, as well as the things mentioned above, make up a succulent list. This book is full of recipes to make your meat go as far as possible.

But there is one word of warning. The cardinal rule for all such things is: *don't ruin what you've got*. Don't put so many bread crumbs in your meat loaf that you don't know it has any meat in it. Don't water down your gravy so that your hash or meat pie has no taste. Choose a recipe compatible with the ingredients you have. A meat pie with gravy is delicious, but so is a curry over rice, which requires no gravy. Don't try to make a meat loaf for six people with half a pound of ground beef. But you can make turnovers for six with it. Parlay a little cold cooked beef into a salad with green peas and then serve a large dish of scalloped potatoes or batter bread to go with it. You won't have any complaints. But if you try to put over that same beef in a watery hash — that's an unhappy meal.

Be sure, too, that the things you put together go well together. I think it is wise to follow recipes until you have a good deal of experience. But even so, it is wise to adapt a recipe you have already used, so that you can imagine it in its new form.

****

V

Beef

****

Ground Beef in Sauces

GROUND BEEF is made into many delicious sauces to be served over spaghetti or other pasta, rice or mashed potatoes; or used to make pinwheels, turnovers and the like. Most have a suggested accompaniment, but you may want to try using them interchangeably.

Spaghetti Sauce (Pasta, p. 32)

1 pound ground beef	both cans full of water
1 large onion, coarsely chopped	1 teaspoon basil
2 cloves garlic, mashed	¼ teaspoon oregano
2 tablespoons oil	pinch rosemary
10½-ounce can tomato purée	salt and pepper
6-ounce can tomato paste	

Sauté onion and garlic in oil until onion is soft. Turn heat to medium high and add ground beef. Stir constantly, breaking it up fine, until beef is browned. Add the rest of the ingredients, stir well and bring to a boil. Reduce heat and simmer slowly, covered, for 1 to 2 hours. Add more boiling water if needed. You can serve this after the first half hour, but it is much better cooked longer.

This is also good made with small cubes of beef instead of ground beef. The procedure is just the same. The Italians call this Spaghetti al Ragu.

Chili con Carne with Beans

1 pound ground beef
2 tablespoons oil
1 large onion, coarsely chopped
2 cloves garlic, mashed
1 tablespoon parsley
salt

1-pound can tomatoes, pieces
  broken up, or substitute (see
  p. 130)
1 tablespoon chili powder
1-pound can red beans, drained
  and rinsed

The directions for this are just the same as for spaghetti sauce, p. 63. Serve over Boiled Rice I (see p. 13).

Greek Turnovers

1 pound ground beef
2 tablespoons margarine
2 onions, coarsely chopped
2 cloves garlic, mashed
1 teaspoon salt
pepper to taste
1½ teaspoons curry powder

½ teaspoon allspice
pinch to ¼ teaspoon cinnamon,
  to taste
1 6-ounce can tomato paste
1 cup water
plain pastry (1½ times recipe,
  p. 126)

Sauté the spices along with the onion. Otherwise the directions for making the sauce are just the same as for spaghetti sauce, p. 63, but it need not cook more than 20 minutes. During this time, make the pastry (see p. 126) and roll out very thin, rolling about a third or fourth of the dough at a time. Make turnovers fairly small, as this is highly seasoned. If you want larger ones, make more pastry and roll it thicker. For detailed instructions for putting together the turnovers, see p. 77.

Keema

¾ pound ground beef
2 tablespoons margarine
1 medium onion, finely chopped
2 cloves garlic, mashed
1 tablespoon coriander seeds
1 teaspoon ground turmeric

1½ teaspoons salt
½ teaspoon chili powder
1 cup canned tomatoes
1 cup fresh peas, or ½ 10-ounce
  package, frozen

Sauté onions in margarine until soft. Mash garlic and coriander seeds together, add to the onion, and cook a few minutes more. Add turmeric, chili powder and salt, and stir and sauté a few minutes more. Now add tomatoes, breaking them up as you add them, and cook all together a while longer. Add ground beef, breaking it up fine, and simmer 30 minutes. Finally add green peas and simmer the whole mixture 20 minutes longer. This is a delightful and different way to use ground beef (lamb may be substituted). Serve over Boiled Rice I (see p. 13).

Other Sauces

Other sauces using ground beef are easy to invent, combining the flavors suggested by any of the recipes for beef, such as meat balls, pot roasts, pilaffs. You would usually start by sautéing onions or garlic in fat until onions are soft. Then add ground beef, breaking it up fine and stirring over fairly high heat until browned. Add the same amount of flour as of fat at this time, if you want the sauce thickened, and cook a few minutes. Then add enough liquid to make a sauce (see p. 100 for directions and proportions for sauce). The liquid should be stock or some substitute (see p. 103), or tomato juice. Season as suggested above. Be sure the seasonings and the liquid for the sauce go well together; for example, if you are using tomato juice, then seasonings should be chosen from a recipe that calls for tomato.

Meat Balls and Meat Loaves

These are generally composed, to begin with, of ground meat, crumbs of some kind (see p. 129), liquid (usually water in these recipes), and seasonings. The proportions are usually 2 cups (1 pound) ground beef, or other meat, to ½ cup liquid.

Often vegetables of one kind or another will be added, and if so, in order to be thoroughly cooked when the meat is done, they must be grated or ground or chopped very fine, or cooked first.

If you boil them before adding, like carrots, be sure to add the cooking water too, as part or all of the liquid called for.

If you add onions or mashed garlic, sauté them in margarine first, and then add them, along with the margarine, to the mixture.

You may want to sauté the garlic, with or without onions, and then remove the garlic. The flavor, or some of it, will go along with the margarine.

Plain Meat Balls

1 pound ground beef	salt and pepper
½ cup toast crumbs	1 teaspoon parsley or chervil
½ cup water	bacon grease, or other fat, for
1 small onion, grated	sautéing

Combine these ingredients in a bowl and knead well. The mixture should be light and springy (add a bit more water if necessary). Shape into flattened balls, and then brown on both sides in a little fat. Reduce heat and sauté slowly until they are cooked through, about 10 to 20 minutes, depending on the size of meat balls you want.

Meat Balls with Cumin

1 pound ground beef	½ to 1 teaspoon ground cumin
1 clove garlic, mashed	1 medium onion, grated
1 tablespoon margarine	salt and pepper
1 teaspoon soy sauce	½ cup toast crumbs
juice of ½ lemon	oil or other fat, for sautéing
water	

Sauté garlic in margarine a few minutes. Put soy sauce and lemon juice in a measuring cup and add enough water to make ½ cup liquid. Put all the rest of the ingredients in a mixing bowl and add melted margarine, after removing the garlic; then add the liquid. Knead the mixture well and proceed as with plain meat balls.

Minted Meat Balls

1 pound ground beef	½ teaspoon dried mint
1 tablespoon margarine	¼ teaspoon oregano
1 clove garlic, mashed	½ cup water
1 small onion, grated	salt and pepper
1 teaspoon vinegar	2 tablespoons oil, or other fat, for
2 teaspoons parsley	sautéing

Sauté garlic in margarine a few minutes. Remove and discard the garlic if you don't want much garlic flavor. Mix all ingredients but oil in a bowl, adding the garlicky margarine, and knead until light. Proceed as with plain meat balls.

Meat Loaf My Way

2 pounds ground beef	1 cup toast crumbs
1 large carrot, in small cubes	another ½ cup water
½ cup water	1 tablespoon parsley
1 onion, chopped fine	¼ teaspoon thyme leaves
1 clove garlic, mashed	¼ teaspoon nutmeg
2 tablespoons margarine	salt and pepper

Simmer carrots in ½ cup water 15 to 20 minutes. Sauté onions and garlic in margarine. Put all the rest of the ingredients in a mixing bowl. Add sautéed onions and garlic, and the carrots with the water they boiled in (making a total of 1 cup water). Knead all this together. It should be light and springy. If not, add a bit more water. Put in a loaf pan about 9 x 5 x 4 inches, and bake, uncovered, about 1 hour at 350°. (To heat over, add some sliced onions, some in the juice and some on top. Heat, covered, at 350° about 45 minutes.)

Meat Loaf with Tomatoes and Green Peppers

2 pounds ground beef	1 cup toast crumbs
1 onion	1 teaspoon parsley
1 green pepper	½ teaspoon basil
1-pound can tomatoes	salt and pepper

If you have a grinder, put the onion and pepper through it. (Crumbs may be made with it too — do that first.) Otherwise, chop the onions and pepper as fine as possible. Put in mixing bowl and add tomatoes, breaking them up, and the juice from the can. Then add the rest of the ingredients. Mix well and put into a loaf pan about 9 x 5 x 4 inches. Bake, uncovered, at 375° about 1½ hours. (To heat over, follow directions in the preceding recipe.)

Ground Beef Cooked with Rice

These recipes make a kind of pilaff. The two suggested here are delicious. You may invent others, starting perhaps with combinations of ingredients suggested by some of the other beef recipes.

Directions for cooking them would be the same for all. Sauté onion or garlic or both in fat until onion is soft. Any spices (not herbs) may be sautéed at the same time. Then turn up heat a little and add ground beef, breaking it up in the pan as fine as possible. When this is brown, add all other ingredients but the rice and mix well. Bring to a boil, add rice and stir up once. Reduce heat to low and simmer, covered, until done (see Boiled Rice II, p. 13), about 30 minutes.

Pilaff with Ground Beef, Tomatoes and Green Pepper

1 pound ground beef
2 tablespoons margarine
1 to 2 onions, coarsely chopped
1 clove garlic, mashed
1 small green pepper, coarsely chopped

1-pound can tomatoes
water added to tomato juice from can to make 2½ cups
1 cup raw long-grain rice
1 tablespoon parsley
salt and pepper

Cook as in directions under Ground Beef Cooked with Rice.

Ground Beef and Rice Casserole

1 pound ground beef
1 small onion, finely chopped
1 tablespoon margarine
1 tablespoon salt pork, finely chopped and sautéed with onion
¼ teaspoon ground allspice

¼ teaspoon thyme leaves
3 to 4 tablespoons tomato paste and 2½ cups water, or equivalent in canned tomatoes plus enough water to make 2½ cups liquid
1 cup raw long-grain rice

Cook as in directions under Ground Beef Cooked with Rice, p. 68.

Ground Beef in Casseroles

These two recipes are good, quick to put together, and you can go off and leave them for long periods.

Ground Beef and Cabbage Casserole

1 pound ground beef
½ large head or one small head of cabbage, coarsely grated

4 to 6 potatoes, peeled and sliced
salt and pepper
1½ cups milk

Put half the grated cabbage in a greased baking dish, then half the potatoes and finally half the ground beef, seasoning each layer with salt and pepper. Repeat. Pour in the milk and bake, covered, for 2 hours at 350°.

Ground Beef and Vegetable Casserole

1 pound ground beef
4 to 6 potatoes, peeled and sliced
3 stalks celery, coarsely chopped
1 green pepper, coarsely chopped
2 medium onions, coarsely chopped

1-pound can tomatoes
salt and pepper
1 tablespoon parsley
⅛ teaspoon thyme leaves

In a greased baking dish put ground beef and vegetables in layers, seasoning each layer with salt and pepper and parsley. Have the tomato on top and sprinkle over the thyme. Bake, covered, for 2 hours at 350°.

Pot Roasts

Pot roasts may be cooked either on top of the stove or in the oven. To cook on top of the stove, brown the meat first in hot fat over medium-high heat. Remove the beef, when brown, to a plate and add onions to the pot to brown. (If the gravy is to be thickened, add flour at this point and cook a few minutes.) Then add flavoring vegetables (add the vegetables that are to be part of the dinner later), liquid (usually water), and return roast to pan. Add all other seasonings, cover and simmer for at least 3 hours (for a 3-to-5 pound roast). You may add carrots or potatoes to some of these recipes (noted as optional in the list of ingredients) to make the whole meal; add them one hour before serving. The potatoes may be quartered, or halved, or left whole, depending on their size (no more than 2 inches in diameter in the pan). The roast may be turned over and salted about halfway through the cooking. Add boiled water as necessary while this is cooking. There should be an inch or so of gravy at the bottom of the pot.

To cook a pot roast in the oven, season it with pepper and other flavorings (except salt) and put the flavoring vegetables (see above) around or on it. Add about a cup of water, put top on the pot and cook in a 350° oven for about 3 hours (for a 3-to-5 pound roast). An hour before serving, salt the roast. Vegetables like carrots and potatoes may be added at this time (see above) to some of the roasts to make a whole meal. Add boiled water as necessary while this is cooking. You should have an inch or so of gravy at the end.

I usually cook enough roast to last three or four days and add extra vegetables to make the whole meal only on the second day. Be sure to put on the table only what you want to serve that day, otherwise you may not have enough for other meals. See pp. 72–74 for directions for heating over pot roasts, and recipes for leftover roast.

Pot Roast My Way

3 to 5 pounds beef chuck, or other cheap cut
2 onions, sliced
2 carrots, cut in 1-inch pieces
1 stalk celery with leaves, cut in 1-inch pieces
1 to 2 tablespoons parsley
¼ to ½ teaspoon thyme leaves
1 to 2 large cloves garlic

1 to 2 cloves
1 to 2 bay leaves
pepper
nutmeg, a light grating
1 cup water
salt
potatoes and more carrots (optional)

Cook according to general directions above.

Pot Roast with Green Peppers

3 to 5 pounds beef chuck, or other cheap cut
1 to 3 green peppers, sliced
1 onion, sliced
1 large clove garlic
1 tablespoon parsley
pepper
1 cup water
salt
potatoes (optional)

Cook according to general directions above.

Pot Roast Lorraine

3 to 5 pounds beef chuck, or other cheap cut
1 cup dried prunes, put under the roast
1 to 2 large onions, coarsely chopped
2 tablespoons flour
2 cups hot water
3 to 6 stalks celery, cut in 1-inch pieces
4 to 8 carrots, quartered
2 to 3 teaspoons parsley
celery leaves
salt and pepper
4 to 6 potatoes (optional)

Cook on top of the stove according to general directions above. Be sure to add all ingredients but the potatoes to the pot when you return the roast to it.

Spicy Pot Roast

3 to 5 pounds beef chuck, or other cheap cut
1 tablespoon margarine
1 tablespoon flour
2 cups hot water
salt and pepper
½ teaspoon each ground allspice, mace, cloves
1 onion, sliced thin
3 bay leaves
4 tablespoons oil
2 tablespoons vinegar

Make a brown roux (see p. 100) with margarine and flour, and add water to make sauce (see p. 100). Mix salt and pepper and spices and rub into beef. Put beef and sauce into pot, add all other ingredients, and proceed according to general directions above. Do not brown beef.

Pot Roast with Tomatoes and Horseradish

3 to 5 pounds beef chuck, or other cheap cut

1 tablespoon margarine and 1 tablespoon oil

1 onion, coarsely chopped

1 pound can tomatoes, or a bit less

1 tablespoon prepared horseradish

juice of ½ lemon

1 small green pepper, sliced

1 teaspoon prepared mustard

salt and pepper

Cook according to general directions above.

This is a particularly good recipe to use for Swiss Steak, too.

Heating Over Pot Roasts

The first rule for heating over anything is that something new should be added, preferably something fairly flavorful. This will keep most things, including pot roasts, from having a leftover taste. The simplest thing to use for most pot roasts is an onion, peeled and quartered. You will often need to add some boiling water, also, to keep the roast from getting too dry.

If potatoes were cooked with the pot roast, remove any that were left. Potatoes cannot be heated over by any ordinary method without tasting hopelessly leftover. However, potatoes from a pot roast can be used to very good advantage, cold, in a meat salad, or with kippered herrings and pickle.

When heating anything over, it is important to cook it all the way through, to keep bacteria from developing. When I heat over my pot roast, I simply add an onion, quartered, about one cup of boiling water, and bake (in oven at 350°) or simmer, covered, for 1 hour, usually adding potatoes and possibly carrots, depending on the recipe.

If you are afraid you have kept it too long, use your nose and throw it out if necessary. Otherwise be sure it is *thoroughly* cooked again.

Hash, or Other Dishes with Leftover Beef

General Directions

There are several important things to remember about leftover beef, in addition to not letting it spoil (see above).

1. Always add some new flavor or ingredient (see above).

2. Meats cooked in moist heat, braised, simmered or boiled, can be recooked or reheated in any way you like. Save as much gravy from original dish as possible for use in these dishes.

3. Do not cut up the meat until you are ready to use it. If you are making hash, cut it into small cubes, about ¼ to ⅜ inch. Cut away all gristle and fat. This is very important, as they are disagreeable in hash, pies or whatever, and will make the dish something to be dreaded rather than to be looked forward to, as it should be.

4. Don't use water in hash, or in sauces for pies, pinwheels or the like. If you do not have good stock (chicken stock is all right) or gravy, use tomatoes or tomato juice if that will go well with what you have. Sometimes milk will augment what gravy you have, as in the recipe for meat pie with leftover beef and gravy. Good stock to augment gravy can be made by boiling bones left from the roast.

5. Hash may be served with, or over, mashed potatoes, rice, toast, pancakes (good, especially if hash is a bit short), hot biscuits or noodles. It may also be baked in the oven with biscuit rounds on top — 20 minutes in a 400° oven.

6. Other offshoots of hash are pies, shepherd's pie, turnovers and pinwheels. These are not always made with leftover beef, but they are a delicious way to use it, along with pastry, mashed potatoes or biscuit dough. If you don't have much meat left, turnovers or pinwheels are indicated, using biscuit dough (see p. 26). The sauce for these is usually thickened.

7. To prepare meat mixture for hashes or other dishes with leftover meat: Sauté onions or garlic or both, and any other vegetables to be used, in margarine or other fat until soft. Then, if you wish the mixture thickened, add flour and cook a few minutes. The

proportions for a medium-thick sauce will be 2 tablespoons flour to 2 tablespoons fat and 1 cup liquid (reduce flour if you want a thinner sauce). Then add liquid, gradually if you are making a thickened sauce, and all other ingredients. Cook together long enough for flavors to blend, and, if you've kept the beef longer than a day or two, long enough to make it safe to eat. Thirty minutes of simmering should be long enough to make it safe when the meat is cut up small. This cooking time will be the time you simmer the sauce, plus the time it is cooked with its accompaniment (for example, in oven with biscuits on top). If the recipe calls for pickles or horseradish, add them at the last minute and do not boil or simmer after adding them. They may not be used, therefore, in any dish which must be baked in the oven, like a pie.

8. If the original roast from which you are making the hash had a very distinctive flavor, like a Spicy Pot Roast, continue with those ingredients in making the hash.

Beef Miroton, or Hash with Pickles

2 cups cooked beef
2 tablespoons margarine or other fat
1 large onion, coarsely chopped
1 tablespoon flour
1 cup stock, or substitute
½ cup canned tomatoes
salt and pepper

2 teaspoons parsley
2 teaspoons vinegar
¼ cup sliced dill pickles
1 teaspoon horseradish (optional)
½ teaspoon dry mustard, mixed with 1 teaspoon vinegar (optional)

Use horseradish and mustard only if needed for flavor. Proceed according to general directions above.

Beef Hash with Tomato

2 cups cooked beef
1 onion, coarsely chopped
1 clove garlic, mashed
2 tablespoons margarine
2 tablespoons flour

2 cups stock or gravy, or combination
2 tablespoons tomato paste or substitute (see p. 130)
1 tablespoon parsley

Proportions of stock or gravy to tomato may be varied, but it is much better with at least some beef stock or gravy. Proceed according to general directions above.

Southern Hash

2 cups cooked beef
2 tablespoons bacon grease or other fat
1 large onion, coarsely chopped
1 stalk celery, cut small

1 green pepper, coarsely chopped
1 to 2 cups gravy, stock or substitute, or combination
salt and pepper

Cook according to general directions above.

Meat Pies

For meat pies, leftover beef may be made using the general directions above, or the recipe given below. Directions for making the pastry will be found on p. 126. Directions for handling the pastry are given in the following recipe, which I want to give in toto as a variation because it is so good and so cheap and filling:

For four people use a small deep oven dish. (Mine is 2 inches deep and barely holds 3½ cups water.) Line it with pastry. Slice 2 large potatoes ⅜-inch thick. Slice a small onion very thin. Slice the beef ¼-inch thick and cut into bite-sized pieces. Put in a layer of half the potatoes, a layer of half the onion, sprinkle on about 2 teaspoons flour, add salt and pepper and then put on a layer of half the beef. Repeat. Add more potatoes if your pan is not filled up. Now put your leftover gravy in a measuring cup and fill the cup up with milk. Pour into the pie. Add more milk if it doesn't come within ¼-inch of top. Wet down the rim of the pastry lining so that the top will stick to it. Cover the pie with pastry, trim it and crimp the edges with a fork. Cut a small hole about ½ inch square in the top to let the steam escape. Bake at 375° about one hour.

This takes longer to describe than to do. If you have remembered to leave the margarine for the pastry out of the refrigerator to soften, you can make both the pastry and the whole pie in 30 to 40 minutes, not counting baking time. This is just delicious, and will make a very satisfying meal.

Pinwheels

This is the recipe to choose if you have very little meat left over. The proportion of dough to meat is very high. Pinwheels are awfully good, however.

Prepare the meat mixture according to the general directions for hash, p. 73, using ingredients suggested by one of the recipes for hash or ground beef in sauce (pp. 63–65), or just plain beef heated in a thickened gravy (add a little onion to keep it from tasting left over).

Roll out dough (I just use biscuit dough, p. 26) rather thin, about ⅜ inch, and into as square a shape as you can. Cover the dough with the meat and part of the sauce or gravy, leaving ½ inch on each side uncovered. Roll up dough into a cylinder and then slice it into ¼-inch slices, to make the pinwheels. Put these on a cookie sheet or any flat pan and bake at 450° about 12 minutes, or until dough is cooked. Serve some of the sauce or gravy over each pinwheel.

Shepherd's Pie

This is made with mashed potatoes combined with one well-beaten egg, instead of pastry or biscuit dough.

The meat mixture is the same as for any of these recipes for hash or pinwheels, pp. 74–75. Put the meat mixture in a baking dish, after simmering it long enough for flavors to blend and to make it safe to eat (see general instructions, p. 73). Cover the top with mashed potatoes or, if you don't want to use quite as much potato as that would take, put mashed potatoes around the edges. Bake in a 425° oven long enough for everything to be thoroughly hot, and the potatoes a little bit browned at edges and peaks, about 20 minutes.

Vegetables may be added to the meat mixture for variety, or to make a whole meal out of the pie. Cook right in with the meat mixture until they are about done before putting the pie in the oven. Of course leftover vegetables may be used as well.

Turnovers

This is another excellent way to use either meat in small quantities or meat that is highly seasoned. You may vary the proportions of meat to pastry by rolling the dough thick (¼ inch) or thin (¹⁄₁₆ inch or less). If you don't have much meat, roll the turnovers thick and big — 4 inches square and ¼ inch thick. These are really good even if there is a lot more pastry than meat. Use biscuit dough (p. 26) for these.

If there is more meat, and it is highly seasoned, I like them small and rolled out thin. Smaller ones may be rolled out 2 inches across and 3 inches long. Use pastry dough (p. 126) for these.

Prepare the meat mixture according to general directions for hash, p. 73, using seasonings suggested by the recipes for hash or for ground beef in sauce (pp. 63–65). These may also be made with ground beef instead of leftover beef.

You are going to turn one side of the pastry over on the other side, and seal the open edges, with the meat mixture inside. If you are using a 4-inch square of pastry, fold over to make a triangle. For pastry cut 2 by 3 inches, put short sides together. Before folding the pastry over, put a small amount of meat mixture, just enough to comfortably fit in the little envelope you are making, leaving space around the open edges so they can be sealed together. Wet the edges and stick them together carefully so they won't leak.

Bake in a 400° oven until pastry is done and a little browned, about 10 minutes.

Leftover Beef with Beans

Not a hash, of course, but a good way to use a small amount of cooked beef.

1 cup cooked beef	1 slice bacon (ends and pieces are
1 cup dried Great Northern beans,	fine for this)
cooked by general directions	leftover gravy
for Cooked Beans, p. 6	juice from cooking beans
1 onion, coarsely chopped	2 tablespoons vinegar
1 clove garlic, mashed	a little mustard, if needed*

* If beef or gravy lack flavor, you may wish to incorporate a little mustard into the vinegar.

The total cooking time for the beans will be about 2 hours. The rest of the dish may be prepared at any time during that period, and the beans can finish cooking along with everything else. Sauté the bacon and remove from the pan. Sauté onion and garlic in the bacon grease until soft. Add beef, beans (these may be completely cooked, if desired), any leftover gravy, enough juice to bring the liquid to the top of the mixture and the vinegar. Add the bacon. Put in 400° oven for at least 20 minutes, or longer if necessary to finish cooking beans. Lower the temperature for a longer baking time.

Beef and Green Pea Salad

Another good way to use a little leftover beef.

1 cup or more cooked beef	½ teaspoon dried mint
1-pound can green peas	½ teaspoon celery salt
salad dressing	pepper
prepared mustard	

Dice the beef small. Mix with drained peas and the dressing (this should be a "boiled" dressing, commercial or homemade, see p. 105). Add seasonings and toss gently so as not to break up peas. Serve cold. Garnish, if you wish, with lettuce or parsley, or some leaves from a bunch of celery. To make a whole meal, serve with something substantial, like batter bread or muffins.

Steaks and Stews

Cheap cuts of beef are often cut as stews or steaks. Actually it is frequently cheaper to buy a piece of chuck and cut it up yourself for stew. (I think I'd let the butcher cut the steaks.) The larger pieces are usually cheaper per pound, and any bone you have left will go nicely in soups or to make stock, or cooked with beans. The same recipes given for pot roasts may be used for stews and steaks.

Pot Roast My Way is about the same as a simple version of Beef Bourguignonne, the classic French stew. You brown the beef cubes in bacon grease or other fat over fairly high heat. When meat is brown, add coarsely chopped onions and let them brown.

Then add 2 tablespoons flour and stir until beef is coated. Reduce heat and add 2 cups water and the seasonings given in the roast recipe, scaled down to the smaller amount of beef (I use one pound for about five people). Simmer for an hour and then add carrots and potatoes and salt and cook another hour. There you have a whole meal. Use other pot roast recipes for stews, too, adapting them the same way. The Spicy Pot Roast recipe (p. 71) is especially good to adapt this way.

I'm including a recipe for Country Steak, because it is a little different from any of the Pot Roast Recipes — it's really like a plain pot roast — but this will give you an idea of how to proceed with cheap steaks. Omit the flour or not, and use any of the recipes given for pot roast, scaling down the seasonings to go with the smaller amount of beef.

Country Steak

I had this at one of the best meals I ever ate. I arrived in a small hotel in south Georgia after a long trip and they served it to me with hot biscuits and buttermilk. That was twenty-seven years ago, but I remember it perfectly, still.

You can use any kind of cheap steak for this. Dredge it with flour and then pound it unmercifully with a mallet, or failing that, the side of a saucer. Dredge it again with flour. Heat 2 tablespoons bacon grease, or other fat, in a large frying pan and brown floured steak well on both sides. Add salt and pepper, and enough water to come up to ⅛ to ¼ inch in the pan. Cover and simmer until the meat almost falls apart, 2 to 3 hours, depending on the type and thickness of the steak. If too much of the liquid cooks away, add boiled water. This makes delicious gravy and is particularly good with mashed potatoes.

Egyptian Lima Bean Stew

½ to 1 pound any cheap cut of beef
1 pound dried lima beans
¼ cup oil

4 cloves garlic
salt to taste
2 teaspoons coriander seeds

This is an excellent way to use dried lima beans, though other beans may be substituted. It has a delicious flavor, and the cheapest cut of beef, such as shank or plate, may be used. Put the bone in with the meat and beans. Soak lima beans overnight if necessary (see p. 6). Next day brown beef in the oil. Use less oil if beef is fat. Add garlic, mashed, and sauté until brown. Immediately turn in beans and soaking water (garlic will turn from brown to black very quickly). Add salt and coriander and simmer for 2 hours, covered. Let most of the water cook away. The beans are good mushy, so boil fast at the end, if necessary.

Boiling a Cut of Beef (Pot-au-Feu)

Up until now, anything sold as a roast in a supermarket or one of the large grocery chains could be cooked as a pot roast, that is, braised. Grades of beef too tough to cook that way simply have not been for sale in such stores. There *is* beef too tough to braise, though, which you will know if you have been given beef locally raised by a non-expert, or if you have ever shopped in foreign markets. I have braised a cut of beef until it turned into strings, but it never got tender. For beef like that, boiling is the answer, and surprisingly enough, beef boiled properly and then served cold, cut into elegant thin slices, is perfectly delicious. The French have been doing it since the time of Henry IV: their famous pot-au-feu.

Pot-au-feu is cheap; it provides you with a wonderful "roast" (or English "joint" — a large piece of beef to be carved at the table or in the kitchen which will be the high point of a festive meal); and the consommé it produces is wonderful as a soup or as the basis for many fine gravies or sauces. There is only one drawback: it is time consuming. I would not recommend starting one at the end of a day's work. But it is fun and rewarding if you are at home at least part of a day and can be in and out of the kitchen fairly often. For about six months, once, I lived in a town where meat as tough as that I described above was all I could afford, and I made a pot-au-feu every Saturday. In addition to the beef and bones, I cooked a chicken and a large piece of beef sausage in it, producing a marvelous flavor in all. We ate the chicken Saturday night, the sausage for lunch a day or two later and the "roast" for

1 to 4 days, depending on the size of the piece of beef. The consommé made sauces all week, if I could keep the family from drinking it up as soup — you need to take a firm stand there. Because the beef is so good cold, it means that you have cooked the meat for up to six meals all at once, a particular boon in the summer. Here it is:

1 to 4 pounds beef or veal	thyme
beef or veal bones	bay leaf
water	cloves
carrots, cut in 1-inch pieces	garlic
onions, left whole	salt and pepper
celery with leaves, cut in 1-inch pieces	1 piece hard sausage like salami (optional, but it adds a wonderful flavor)
1 turnip, left whole	1 chicken (optional)
1 parsnip (optional)	
parsley	

You should have about equal weight of beef and bones, unless you add the chicken or sausage. If you add both, you can make a good pot-au-feu with only about 1 pound beef, say, to 4 pounds bones. The bones give body to the consommé and make it jell. I have not given amounts for vegetables and seasonings because that depends on the size of the pot-au-feu. You can be guided by the proportions in Pot Roast My Way (p. 70) in deciding the amounts. Put beef and bones in cold water to cover, and a bit more to take care of later additions, and bring gradually to a boil. It is important for it to come to a boil slowly, as you want the beef flavor to seep into the consommé. You will use every drop of that and there will be no waste. When the pot-au-feu begins to boil, a scum will rise to the top. If you want beautiful clear consommé, take every bit of it off and save to put in soup or another dish. I just leave mine alone. When it comes to a rolling boil, add the vegetables and seasonings, and sausage if used, adding salt cautiously. Add more boiling water to cover if necessary. Let this simmer all together about 4 hours. If you cook a chicken with this, leave enough room for it from the beginning, but do not add it until 1½ hours before the cooking is over.

Serve chicken hot, but allow the beef to cool before serving. The vegetables have given their all and are pretty tasteless, but I always called the children into the kitchen while I bottled the consommé and we ate them up. When it is cool enough to handle, pour the consommé into clean bottles and refrigerate (a funnel with a sieve or strainer the same size is handy for this). If you want to eat the consommé cold (makes a nice jellied consommé if you had enough bones in the pot) do so within about 36 hours. If more time than that has passed, be sure that it boils at least 20 minutes before you use it. If you have any left that you don't want for sauces, it makes a fine soup with small pasta cooked in it.

This is not something to be undertaken casually, at least not often. But it can be a part of your life on a regular basis of some kind, to the very good advantage of your budget *and* the people you cook for. It is quite delicious enough to squander a nice piece of brisket or round in, if you want to plunge, but the real point is that any beef — or any I have ever seen — no matter how tough, is a real treat cooked this way.

****

VI

Pork

****

COOKING PORK is quite a different business from cooking beef. To begin with, it is all tender, but since it must be thoroughly done larger cuts must have long cooking anyway. Any of it may be roasted in an open pan, however, just plain with salt and pepper. Of course, better cuts will taste better, but it is all tender. Also you can usually judge the quality by the price, and this is not always possible for beef. Chuck beef is cheap because it is tough unless it is properly cooked. But since all pork is tender and can generally be cooked in any way you like, the price is usually tied directly to the quality of the meat.

For the same reasons there are a lot fewer specific recipes for pork in this book than there are for beef. It is so much easier to cook, and sausage tastes like sausage no matter what you do with it (though a good taste, for all that). I've confined myself to fresh pork roasts, ham and leftovers, and sausage. But here are some extra suggestions:

Cook a picnic ham, either to begin with or the second time you serve it, right in with dried pinto beans. It's a very good combination and you can satisfy an enormous crowd with it.

For beans and franks, sauté some celery, onion and green peppers. Add beans to this and mix well, and put franks on top. Bake.

Cook backbone with dumplings like chicken and dumplings. Backbone is sometimes called "spare ribs — country style."

Cook bacon (ends and pieces) or salt pork, potatoes and snap beans together country style, with just enough water to simmer them in. Parboil pork if you wish to make it less greasy. Season with a lot of pepper.

Cook leftover pork like Leftover Beef with Beans (p. 77). Or devil it: use 3 tablespoons margarine, 1 teaspoon prepared mustard, 1 teaspoon lemon juice or vinegar, 2 teaspoons Worcestershire sauce, and any gravy you have left over, and heat pork in this. Another good pork hash: mix pork with diced onions, 2 cloves, good pinch of sage, thyme leaves, 3 or 4 juniper berries, crushed, 2 tablespoons vinegar, stock, and salt and pepper. See instructions for making beef hash (pp. 73–74) for guidelines.

Brown sausage patties and bake with cooked beans (p. 6), or lentils. Onions, sage, thyme and maybe some canned tomato or tomato juice are good seasonings for this. (Lentils are good this way, cooked as on p. 10 and then baked plain with sausage patties. Add a little of the cooking liquid.)

Bake browned sausage patties on top of sliced potatoes, well seasoned, and layered with onion rings, adding just enough water to come to the bottom of the top layer of potatoes.

Roast Pork

I like a pork roast (what I buy is usually a shoulder, or fresh picnic ham) braised rather than dry roasted. Put it into the oven with salt and pepper to taste (on and around it), 1 tablespoon parsley and ⅛ to ¼ teaspoon thyme leaves sprinkled around it, one onion, sliced, and a cup of water. Bake, covered, 3 to 3½ hours at 350° (3½ hours is long enough for a 6½-pound shoulder — pork should be thoroughly done). This is very good, and is easy to heat over another day. Just add another cup of water and another onion, sliced or quartered, and heat one hour at 350°. Potatoes, halved or quartered, may be added when reheating, or for the last hour when the roast is first cooked.

Roast Pork with Ginger and Lemon

3-to-4-pound piece of pork   salt and pepper
2 onions, quartered   boiled water
1 teaspoon ginger
juice of ½ lemon, plus one lemon
    slice

Put all the ingredients except the water in a heavy pot or casserole, and bake in a 300° oven 2½ to 3 hours. Look at it from time to time and add boiled water if needed. After you take up the roast, add enough boiling water to make a nice gravy. You should have about a cupful of gravy in all. See directions above to reheat this, adding an onion as suggested.

Braised Pork Roast with Tomato

3-pound pork roast   1 large onion, sliced and halved
⅓ cup brown sugar   ⅓ cup tomato ketchup
salt and pepper   1 cup canned tomatoes
½ cup water

Rub the pork all over with sugar and salt and pepper. Put in a heavy pot or casserole and add the rest of the ingredients. Cover and bake in a 350° oven about 2½ to 3 hours.

A large pork roast like a shoulder, or half a fresh ham, may be cooked like this. It should be cooked about 30 minutes to the pound. To reheat, see recipe above for roast pork. Cooked or canned beans may be added to this the last time it appears, along with a quartered onion and maybe some more ketchup — very good. See p. 6 for cooked beans; if you use canned, rinse them carefully and drain.

Ham

Ordinary commercial ham, which is the only kind that need concern us in this book, does not need a real recipe. Much of it is sold "fully cooked." If you are not certain, ask the butcher. I always bake mine in any case, in a shallow open pan, at least 20 minutes to the pound at 300°, because I like it hard and dry. It should be served cold, when it will make nice thin slices. After you take it up, put some boiling water in the pan and get up all the cooking juices and whatever is stuck to the pan. You may add coffee to this, either cold coffee, or just ½ teaspoon of instant coffee. With or without the coffee, it makes delicious gravy for mashed potatoes or grits.

For economy the ham should be used as the main meat for dinner and not be frittered away in sandwiches. However, I usually cheat and give my family one lunch with ham sandwiches, as they are very popular. Here are some recipes for leftover ham after you have gotten off all the good slices.

Ham and Barbecued Rice

1 to 2 cups cooked ham, diced
1 onion, coarsely chopped
2 tablespoons margarine
1 tablespoon tomato ketchup
2 teaspoons prepared mustard
2 teaspoons Worcestershire sauce

½ teaspoon chili powder
2 cups chicken stock (may be made with bouillon cubes)
1 cup raw, long-grain rice
½ teaspoon salt

Sauté onion in margarine until soft. Add rice as for pilaff (see p. 14), and then add all the rest of the ingredients and cook as for pilaff about 30 minutes.

Creamed Ham on Toast

¾ cup cooked ham, diced
1½ cups cream sauce (see p. 102)
¼ teaspoon prepared mustard

salt and pepper
3 hard-boiled eggs, sliced
6 slices toast

Cut ham off bone and dice small or chop fairly fine. Make the cream sauce and add mustard and salt and pepper. Be careful with the salt; sometimes the ham is quite salty. Stir in ham and mix well, and then stir in sliced eggs carefully to keep as intact as possible. Serve on hot toast.

Red Rice with Ham

This is one of my favorite recipes.

¾ cup to 2 cups cooked ham, diced
1 large onion, coarsely chopped
2 stalks celery, cut fairly fine
2 tablespoons bacon grease, or other fat
1 cup raw, long-grain rice

½ teaspoon salt
½ green pepper, chopped fine
⅛ teaspoon ground sage
pinch thyme leaves
1 28-ounce can tomatoes
1 cup water

Sauté onion and celery in bacon grease until onions are soft. Meanwhile dice ham. Then add ham to pan and brown it a bit. Add rice as for pilaff (see p. 14), add other ingredients and cook as for pilaff, about 30 minutes. A pound can of tomatoes may be substituted for the 28-ounce can; add another ½ cup of water.

For other uses of leftover ham, see
    Ham and Bean Soup, p. 48.
    Split Pea Soup, p. 12.

Sausage

Sausage and Corn Fritters

1 pound bulk sausage
2 cups corn (fresh, canned and drained, or frozen, thawed)
2 eggs, separated
1 cup milk
1 cup flour

1 teaspoon baking powder
1 teaspoon salt
pepper
paprika
oil for frying

Put sausage in a frying pan, break it up and sauté until the pink color has gone. Beat up egg yolks in a mixing bowl, add milk and mix well. Add corn and sausage and mix well again. Sift together flour, baking powder, salt, pepper and paprika. Add to the sausage mixture and mix well again. Fold in stiffly beaten egg whites (see p. 129). Heat a frying pan as hot as for pancakes (see p. 31), about 380° if you have an electric frying pan, and add oil ⅛ to ¼ inch deep. Drop fritter mixture into this by the table-spoonful and flatten each one. Fry until golden brown on both sides, 2 to 4 minutes in all.

Baked Macaroni and Sausage

1 pound bulk sausage	1 teaspoon sugar
2 cups cooked macaroni (p. 32)	1 teaspoon salt
1 large onion, chopped	pepper
1 green pepper, chopped	½ cup bread crumbs (p. 129)
1-pound can tomatoes	

Make the sausage into patties and brown on both sides in a frying pan. Remove. Pour off excess fat, leaving enough to sauté onion and green pepper in. Also pour a little into the oven dish to grease it with. Sauté onions and green pepper until soft. Add tomato (juice and all), sugar, salt and pepper, and cook this sauce for a few minutes. Put half the macaroni in the greased baking dish. Put sausage patties on top. Cover with the rest of the macaroni, and pour sauce over all. Sprinkle with bread crumbs. Bake at 375° for 45 minutes.

Sausage Pie

This is delicious, a special dish, and very cheap.

1 pound bulk sausage	2 tablespoons flour
pastry made with 3 cups flour (p. 126)	2 onions, coarsely chopped
4 to 6 medium potatoes, sliced	1 stalk celery, chopped fine
salt and pepper	hot milk

Make the pastry and line a 2-quart deep dish with about two thirds of it. Lay the sliced potatoes, seasoned with salt and pepper and sprinkled with flour, the onions and the celery, in alternate layers with sausage, made into small patties but left raw. Fill up dish with hot milk, about to the top of the potatoes. Moisten the edges of the pastry and cover the dish with another sheet of pastry made with the rest of the dough. Crimp the edges with the tines of a fork, and cut a small hole in the center of the top pastry so the steam can escape. Bake for 1 hour at 350°.

Toad-in-the-Hole

1 pound bulk sausage	1 egg
1 cup flour	1¼ cups milk
¼ teaspoon salt	

Make a batter with all the ingredients but the sausage. Stir well with a wire whisk. (If you don't have a whisk, add milk slowly to the other batter ingredients and stir until smooth.) Let stand 30 minutes. Meanwhile, shape sausage into patties and brown on both sides in an oven-proof pan. Pour off about half of the fat. Preheat oven to 425°. Pour batter over sausage and remaining grease while it is hot. Put in heated oven and bake for 30 minutes.

****

VII

Chicken

****

THANK GOD for chicken. Here is your Sunday dinner when times are hardest. If you must have the boss to dinner you can be fairly splashy with chicken without ruining the budget. (Chicken Salad, Chicken with Oregano and Garlic, and Spiced Chicken with Rice are all good for this.) If you haven't got much in the house besides chicken, flour and water, Chicken and Dumplings is food for the gods.

Country Captain

This is said to have been a favorite of President Franklin Roosevelt's. At any rate it is a favorite of mine. I like it for birthdays or other high days, but it is a little tricky, I think, if you are going to cook more than one chicken, and so I don't try to use it for company, or did only once.

1 3-to-3½-pound fryer, cut in
　serving pieces
salt
flour
pepper
2 to 3 tablespoons margarine and
　a little oil
½ green pepper, chopped

1 onion, coarsely chopped
1 clove garlic, mashed
1½ teaspoons curry powder, or to
　taste
⅛ teaspoon thyme leaves
1-pound can tomatoes
3 tablespoons raisins

Salt chicken pieces and roll them in flour. Brown in the fat and remove. Add pepper, onion, green pepper, garlic, curry powder and thyme to the remaining fat in the pan. Sauté until onion is soft. Add more margarine if necessary. Return the chicken to the pan and add tomatoes and juice from the can. Simmer, covered, 45 minutes to 1 hour. Add raisins and cook 15 minutes more. Serve with mashed potatoes or noodles.

Chicken and Dumplings

This is a great standby and perfectly wonderful.

1 3-to-3½-pound fryer
5 cups water
salt and pepper (*no other
　seasonings*)

Dumplings (p. 28)

Put chicken and water and salt and pepper in a fairly large pot and bring to a boil. Simmer, covered, about 1½ hours. When it is perfectly tender, take it out and let it cool enough to handle. Roll out dumplings and cook in the chicken broth according to directions for Dumplings. Be sure to roll them very, very thin, as directed, or they will be tough and indigestible. While they are simmering, take chicken off the bones and tear into bite-sized pieces. When dumplings have finished cooking, put chicken back in the pot, heat and serve. This is even more delectable if you cook chicken in good, strained chicken stock.

Chicken Chowder

This is excellent for a rather small amount of leftover chicken. The recipe does not call for stock, but you can make this with even less chicken (½ cup or so) if you make stock out of the leftover bones and skin (see p. 103) and substitute it for the water.

1 cup cooked chicken, diced small	3 large potatoes, peeled and diced
1 onion, coarsely chopped	salt and pepper
2 stalks celery, diced	1 tablespoon flour
2 tablespoons margarine	1 tablespoon margarine
2 cups hot water	1 cup milk

Sauté onions and celery in margarine until soft. Add water, potatoes, salt and pepper, and simmer, covered, about 30 minutes. Now add chicken, and manié "butter" (see p. 101) made from 1 tablespoon flour and 1 tablespoon margarine, and cook until thickened. Add milk and reheat slowly but do not boil. If you have kept the chicken more than a day or two, put it in the chowder with potatoes and water.

Other Ideas for Leftover Chicken

Leftover chicken is good made into pies, pinwheels and turnovers. See pp. 75–77 in the chapter on beef for guidelines. It is also good curried, over rice. See recipe for curry sauce for fish, p. 60, substituting milk for other liquid.

Chicken with Oregano and Garlic

1 3-to-3½-pound fryer, cut in serving pieces	salt
	4 cloves garlic, mashed
3 tablespoons oil (olive oil for company)	pepper
	1 teaspoon oregano

Salt chicken pieces and brown in hot oil. Remove chicken, reduce heat and brown garlic slowly. Add pepper. Return chicken to pot, sprinkle oregano over it, cover and bake at 350° until tender, about 1 hour.

This is delicious. It is very good served with cooked noodles tossed in the pan after taking up the chicken. Add a little boiled water to the pan if necessary to make up enough gravy to coat noodles.

Country, or Smothered, Chicken

This is one of the easiest ways to cook a delicious chicken dish. It isn't elegant, but it's *good*.

1 3-to-3½-pound fryer, whole or
  cut into serving pieces
4 tablespoons flour, about
2 teaspoons salt, about

pepper
4 tablespoons margarine
½ cup water

Turn oven to 450°. Put chicken in a casserole and sprinkle flour and salt and pepper on and around it. Pour melted margarine over it, as evenly as possible. Put in oven, uncovered, 20 minutes. Then add water and cover. Reduce heat to 350° and bake, covered, at least an hour longer, or until very tender. There will be delicious gravy in the bottom of the pot.

Chicken with Rice

There are as many recipes for this as there are cooking styles. The simplest is to cook as for smothered chicken (above), with or without the flour. Forty-five minutes before serving, add about 2 cups boiling water and 1 cup raw, long-grain rice. You will probably need to add about ½ teaspoon salt, but taste it and see. Toward the end check to see if the rice is done. If it is dry but not done, add more boiling water and cook until it is done. If it is done but not dry enough, take off the pan top and cook until dry.

Creole Chicken with Rice

1 3-to-3½-pound chicken, cut in
  serving pieces
3 tablespoons fat
1 onion, coarsely chopped
1 clove garlic, mashed
2 cups water
half of 1-pound can tomatoes
1 slice lemon
1 tablespoon parsley

⅛ teaspoon thyme leaves
1 bay leaf
2 cloves
3 to 4 carrots, quartered
1 large turnip, quartered
2 teaspoons salt, about
1-inch piece red pepper
1 cup raw long-grain rice

Brown chicken in the fat. When almost brown, add onion and garlic and brown slightly. Now add all the rest of the ingredients except the rice. Simmer, covered, about 45 minutes. Then add rice and another ½ teaspoon salt, and simmer, covered, about 45 minutes, or until rice is done (see Chicken with Rice, p. 91).

Chicken Salad

This was one of the most standard dishes to serve for company when I was growing up. I still like to use it. Nearly everybody likes it and most of the work can be done the day before. Serve it in a bed of lettuce or surrounded with fresh parsley on such occasions.

1 3-to-3½-pound fryer	celery (see directions below for
4 to 5 cups water	quantity required)
salt and pepper	enough mayonnaise to moisten
1 tablespoon parsley	the salad
⅛ teaspoon thyme	
leaves	

Put fryer in boiling water and add salt and pepper, parsley and thyme. Simmer until very tender, about 1½ hours. Remove chicken from pan and save broth for soup or other use. When chicken is cool enough to handle, take the meat off the bones, saving skin and bones for second stock (see p. 103). Chill thoroughly. (The chicken may be cooked the day before using it, but do not make the salad until just before serving — chicken and mayonnaise are a very perishable combination.)

To serve, cut up chicken into small dice, roughly ¼ or ⁵⁄₁₆ inch square. Measure the chicken in a measuring cup and put in a mixing bowl. Cut up celery stalks into similar-sized pieces, using enough to make exactly half as much celery as chicken. Moisten with just enough mayonnaise not to have any of the salad dry.

I like this simple version much better than the more elaborate ones.

Spiced Chicken with Rice

1 3-to-3½-pound chicken
4 cups water
1 carrot, quartered
1 onion, halved
1 stalk celery with leaves, halved
2 teaspoons parsley
salt and pepper

1 clove garlic, mashed
1 tablespoon parsley
1 good pinch each of cinnamon, cloves, nutmeg
2 tablespoons margarine
1 cup raw, long-grain rice
2½ cups chicken broth

Simmer chicken in the water, with carrot, onion, celery, 2 teaspoons parsley, salt and pepper, covered, until chicken is just tender, 1 to 1¼ hours. Remove chicken from broth and reserve broth. Tear chicken into bite-sized pieces, saving skin and bones for another day. Sauté garlic, parsley and spices in 2 tablespoons margarine a few minutes. Add rice as for pilaff, p. 14, then 2½ cups of the broth and the chicken. Simmer, covered, about 30 minutes, or until done.

Giblet Rice

It is best, I think, to save the livers for something else. They are not particularly good with rice and are delicious many other ways. Freeze them until you have enough to make a meal, or use them in an omelet. Giblets may also be used many other ways. See the index.

several sets of giblets (hearts, gizzards, necks if included)
2 teaspoons parsley
⅛ teaspoon thyme leaves
salt and pepper

2 tablespoons margarine
1 onion, chopped fine
1 cup raw, long-grain rice
stock from giblets
½ teaspoon poultry seasoning

Bring giblets slowly to a boil in water to cover. Add parsley, thyme, salt and pepper. Reduce heat and simmer, covered, until tender, at least 1 hour. Remove giblets and reserve stock. Cut gristle off from gizzards and chop the gizzard meat and the hearts and the meat from the necks quite fine. Make a pilaff (p. 14), adding the chopped giblets, and using the stock they cooked in plus enough water to make 2½ cups liquid. Season with poultry seasoning.

****

VIII

Variety Meats

****

Brains

Brains are delicious and are one thing that is still cheap. They are very delicate, but rather rich, and are often served over toast. I have never seen any in the stores that were not ready to cook. If you find any that are not, standard cookbooks (the big ones) say to remove the membranes and remove the blood by soaking. This has always been done when I have bought them. You do need to parboil them for about 20 minutes, however. The brains offered for sale in my area are all pork brains, but you should be able to cook any type the same way.

Brains Poulette

Prepare 2 sets of brains (about ½ pound), if necessary, as above. Parboil them in salted water with 2 tablespoons vinegar added for about 20 minutes. Drain them and plunge in cold water. Cut into small pieces and heat in a Poulette Sauce made as follows. Make a roux (see p. 100) with 3 tablespoons margarine and 3 tablespoons flour. Make your sauce (p. 100) by adding chicken stock (you may make this with chicken bouillon cubes) or it may be made with beef stock (no substitute for this), about 1½ cups of either. Beat up 1 egg and add the juice of ½ lemon. Incorporate this (p. 101) in the sauce. A sprinkling of nutmeg may be added. Serve over toast. This is very rich and will serve four to six people.

Sautéed Brains

½ pound brains	3 tablespoons margarine
¼ cup flour	vinegar
salt	chervil or parsley
pepper	

Parboil brains 18 to 20 minutes in water with a little vinegar added (1 tablespoon to the quart). Drain and cover with cold water. Let stand until cool. Dry and roll in flour seasoned with salt and pepper. Sauté over medium heat in margarine until a nice brown. Remove to a warm serving plate and pour the vinegar into the pan. Stir all around and add more margarine if necessary to make a nice sauce. Sprinkle the brains with parsley or chervil and put on toast. Pour margarine and vinegar over them.

Kidneys

These can be very cheap indeed and they are delicious. Lamb and veal kidneys are delicate and can be cooked many ways. Beef kidneys require a little more doing. Nowadays they have usually been skinned, but if not, plunge them in boiling water for a minute, drain, and they are said to be easy to skin. I do it anyway, to be sure they are not smelly. Don't be alarmed if they smell a little bit in the pan — they won't at the table, and they taste great. Slice the kidneys about ¼ inch thick and remove the yellow core before cooking.

Beef Kidney Casserole

a pair of beef kidneys (1 pound or more)	1 teaspoon powdered mushrooms
3 to 4 slices bacon (ends and pieces are fine)	1-pound can tomatoes
	2 onions, sliced
salt and pepper	3 to 4 large potatoes
	stock or substitute (p. 103)

Prepare kidneys as in general directions above. Put the bacon in the bottom of a casserole. Put a layer of kidneys on top, season with salt and pepper and mushroom powder, then a layer of tomato and one of onions. Finally put a thick layer of potatoes over all and salt them. Pour enough stock (almost any kind will do as this is highly flavored) to reach to within three quarters of an inch of the top, cover and bake at 300° for 2½ hours.

Lamb or Veal Kidneys

Prepare kidneys as in general directions above. Sauté a little onion in margarine until soft. Add the kidneys and sauté over low heat until they are done (lose their pink color), about 5 minutes, adding some parsley as they cook.

Make a sauce out of some leftover gravy, to which you may add a teaspoon or so of tomato sauce, or paste or purée. Add this sauce to cooked kidneys in the pan and heat together a few minutes. If you don't have any leftover gravy, add stock made with bouillon cubes, and the tomato. If you wish to thicken it, take pan off stove, add a little cornstarch mixed with cold water, put back on the stove, and simmer at least a minute, stirring constantly. Serve over hot toast.

Instead of this sauce, you may make a roux (see p. 100) and then make a sauce (p. 100) by adding 1 cup stock (may be made with bouillon cubes), ½ teaspoon mustard and ½ teaspoon Worcestershire sauce. Pour over cooked kidneys and let stand a few minutes to blend.

Liver

All liver should be cooked gently and slowly, though it need not be cooked very long, just enough to lose most of its pink color. Calf's liver is good cooked almost any way, but it is very expensive indeed, and beef liver, properly cooked, is very good. Pork liver takes more doing. It's worth it, though, as all kinds of liver are unusually rich in vitamins and iron, and are an excellent source of protein; and pork liver is very cheap indeed. Liver and onions is a combination made in heaven.

Sautéed Beef Liver with Onions

Sauté sliced onions, the more the better — maybe 3 large ones for a pound of sliced liver — in margarine until about soft. Reduce heat to low before adding liver. Now add liver slices to the pan and sauté gently until they lose their pink color (all the way through), seasoning only with pepper. Check to see if they are done by cutting a small corner off a slice; it varies with thickness of slices, pan, etc. If they cook too slowly, raise heat to medium. Salt them when they finish cooking, and serve hot. If cooked slowly, they will be perfectly tender, with a delicious flavor.

Beef Liver and Potato Casserole

This is delicious, with quantities of delicious gravy. If you have a lot of hungry people to serve, you might add a side dish of grits.

1 pound beef liver, cut in slices	6 medium potatoes, sliced
as much bacon, up to 8 slices, as you can afford, using ends and pieces	salt and pepper
	¼ teaspoon sage
	stock to cover
2 medium onions, sliced	

Put layers of liver, bacon, onion slices and potato slices in a greased baking dish, sprinkling salt and pepper and sage on each layer of liver and potatoes. Pour in stock to barely cover the ingredients. Chicken stock made with chicken bouillon cubes does well enough. Bake, covered, for 2 hours at 350°. (You can eat this after 1 hour, but it is not as good.) Let stand 15 minutes for flavors to blend, before serving.

Liver Dinner

Make this as above, using ¼ pound bacon (ends and pieces) and ½ to ¾ pound liver, sliced. Use a pound can of tomatoes instead of stock. Omit the sage and season with 1 tablespoon parsley, 1 bay leaf, ⅛ teaspoon thyme and ½ green pepper, diced (green pepper is optional). This is better if you sauté bacon first, remove bacon to the casserole, dredge liver slices in flour and then sauté them very gently in the bacon grease before adding to the casserole. Bake at 375° for 1 hour.

Sautéed Pork Liver

This is done the same way as beef liver, but be even more careful to sauté it very slowly. Be sure you dry the liver, too, so that it will really sauté, and not just simmer in the juice which has cooked out of it. Simmered pork liver has too strong an iron flavor, I think. This is why I like liver fritters better than liver dumplings (see below). You want your burner, when sautéing liver, just high enough so that it will sauté instead of simmer, and no higher. For the same reason, don't try to cook too much liver in one pan.

Pork liver slices should not be more than ⅜ inch thick for best results, though a little bit thicker isn't too bad. But if the slices hump up in the pan, cut them in half horizontally. Liver is better if it doesn't cook too long. Five minutes on each side on low heat is plenty.

Pork Liver Dumplings and Fritters

There are many recipes for liver dumplings, and the ones I have tried are fairly good. But I think much the same mixture is a lot better made into fritters. It will take a little oil or margarine, but the fritters cook faster, and are more filling. If you are really pinching pennies, you will be using a good deal of margarine anyhow to supply enough calories, but be sure to use up any left in the pan; put it on bread. The fritters are delicious.

Fritter Mixture:

½ pound pork liver
2 tablespoons margarine
1 large onion, coarsely chopped
1 clove garlic, mashed
2 eggs
½ cup milk

4 cups soft crumbs (see p. 129)
¼ cup flour
⅛ teaspoon marjoram
2 teaspoons parsley
salt and pepper

Lay the liver on a chopping board and chop fine with a heavy knife, or put through a meat grinder. Sauté onion and garlic in margarine. Beat up eggs in a mixing bowl. Add liver, sautéed onion and garlic and the rest of the ingredients. Mix well. Drop by tablespoonfuls into a pan hot enough for pancakes (see p. 31) with a film of oil or melted margarine in it. Fry fritters on both sides until brown, about 4 minutes.

For dumplings, reduce eggs to 1, milk to ¼ cup, and add another ¼ cup of flour. Make the mixture the same way as the fritter mixture. To cook, have a large pot of salted water boiling and drop dumplings in by the teaspoonful while the water boils vigorously. (Add more flour if needed to make the dumplings hold together.) When all are in, reduce heat, cover pot and simmer for about 10 minutes. When done, lift out with a slotted spoon and add to soup (or broth or consommé). Don't cook them in the soup, however, or they will take so much of it up you will hardly have any left.

Pork Liver Pâté

This is absolutely delicious spread on toast or crackers. Serve it with a meal and you won't need any other meat. Round out the meal with a hefty casserole like scalloped potatoes (see p. 118).

1 pound pork liver	1 teaspoon parsley
6 ounces lean pork	⅛ teaspoon thyme
6 ounces salt pork fat	¼ teaspoon salt
1 onion	slices of salt pork fat, or slices of
2 teaspoons flour	bacon (ends and pieces are
1 egg	fine)

Put liver, lean and fat pork, and onion through a meat grinder. Put all this in a bowl, add flour and stir vigorously a long time for everything to blend together. Beat egg in a separate bowl and add parsley, thyme and salt. Add this to the liver mixture and mix well. Line a small loaf pan with very thin slices of salt pork, pack liver mixture into this and then cover with more salt-pork slices. Or you may put the liver mixture in a greased oven-proof bowl and cover with bacon slices. Both ways are delicious. Set either pâté pan or bowl in a shallow pan, put in the oven (375°) and pour boiling water into the shallow pan so that it will surround pâté pan. The shallow pan should be deep enough to hold water about 1 to 1½ inches deep. Bake about 2 hours. Chill before using. This keeps well in the refrigerator, and is even better the second or third day.

****

IX

To Make a Sauce

****

FOR ORDINARY HOME use the most common sauces are ones thickened with flour and margarine. These sauces are usually vehicles for meat, fish or vegetables, rather than sauces you put over them. The flour and margarine thickeners are called either a roux or manié "butter," depending on the way you make them. If you add flour directly to a liquid, it lumps, and there really are few things worse than a lumpy sauce. You can, if you want to thicken a gravy for example, put some flour in a cup and add a little gravy to it, and then a little more, stirring constantly, and then put that back in the gravy. But even done that way, it is very hard to keep it from lumping. However, if you combine flour with butter or margarine first, the flour slides right in without lumping.

The roux. If you are starting a sauce of this kind from scratch, you start with a *roux*. Melt margarine in a small frying pan or saucepan, and when it is melted, add flour and a little salt. For a blond roux, do this over low heat and cook the flour in the margarine a few minutes before proceeding to the sauce, but do not brown it. You will use a blond roux for cream and velouté sauces. If a recipe just calls for a "roux," it means a blond roux. For a brown roux you cook the flour in the margarine until it browns. This must not be done over very high heat, though, because if the flour burns it will not thicken the sauce. Gravies are good thickened with a brown roux, and some Espagnole dishes. If you have browned flour on hand, you can make this more easily. Just put some flour in a small shallow pan and put in the oven when you have it going anyway. The flour will keep well in a tightly closed clean jar, and you will be glad to have it when you start to make a hash.

To make the sauce from the roux, add the liquid (milk for cream sauce, stock for velouté, often a combination) and seasonings. The quickest way to do this is to turn the heat up high under the roux and add a little of the liquid, stirring constantly with a wire whisk. As soon as the flour swells up, add a little more liquid and work that in, stirring until it is smooth and thick. Repeat until liquid is used up, or you have the volume and thickness you want. Reduce heat to low as soon as you add the last of the liquid. If you don't have a wire whisk (which will keep it from lumping) you had better do this on a much lower heat. It will take a lot longer to thicken (the whisks are worth their weight in gold) but it won't get lumpy. Add seasonings and whatever else you are going to add to it while the sauce is bubbling. This is the way you make cream (béchamel), velouté and most other household sauces.

Manié "butter." If you want to thicken a sauce you already have, that is, if something is poaching or simmering in a liquid that you want to thicken to make into a sauce, you will use *manié "butter."* In this book we are using margarine, as I do in my kitchen, but I have never seen "manié margarine," so I have gone on calling it manié "butter." This is merely margarine and flour mashed together into a smooth paste. The recipes that call for this give the quantities. The proportions are usually the same as for cream sauce. Add manié "butter" to the liquid and continue simmering until it thickens.

Incorporating an egg. Many recipes call for incorporating an egg or two into the sauce. Eggs will curdle if added to anything which is boiling, or if it is boiled after they are added, so they must be handled carefully. When you are ready for the egg, take the pot you will add it to off the burner. Beat up the egg in a separate bowl. Ladle a little from the pot into the egg and mix well. Repeat several times, then turn egg mixture into the pot and stir well. Put back on the burner, stirring constantly, until it thickens. Do not let it boil. The procedure is the same for incorporating an egg into anything hot — sauce, soup or whatever.

Most specific recipes for sauces are printed in the appropriate places elsewhere in this book. See "Sauces" in the index for these. Here are the two basic ones for our purposes.

Cream Sauce (Béchamel)

2 tablespoons margarine   1 cup milk
2 tablespoons flour   other seasonings
¼ teaspoon salt

Put the sauce together according to the general instructions for sauces, above. The basic sauce calls for just the first 4 ingredients. If you want a thick sauce, add 1 more tablespoon flour. If you want a thin sauce, subtract a tablespoon of flour.

The seasonings in addition to the salt will depend on what you are using the sauce for. Here are a few general suggestions in case you want to experiment.

For fish: 1) onions, garlic, lemon juice, oregano; 2) lemon juice or grated rind, and nutmeg. Vinegar can often be substituted for lemon juice.

For vegetables: 1) peas and beans with savory; 2) cabbage with mustard or dill or Worcestershire sauce; 3) carrots with nutmeg or paprika.

For chicken: 1) poultry seasoning, or chervil and a bit of thyme; 2) onions and sage with a bit of thyme; 3) curry powder with onions.

If you want your sauces seasoned with onions or garlic, sauté them in the margarine before adding the flour, until onions are soft. Garlic can be sautéed right in with the onions, but if garlic alone is used it will need to sauté only a very few minutes.

Leftover fish, chicken or vegetables are good heated over in a well-seasoned cream sauce. I usually sauté onions in the margarine first for this. If you have broth in which the leftovers were cooked, try using half broth and half milk for the liquid.

When you use dry, nonfat milk to make sauces, add a little extra margarine or they will not be rich enough.

Velouté Sauce

2 tablespoons margarine   1 cup stock
2 tablespoons flour   other seasonings
¼ teaspoon salt

Put the sauce together according to the general directions for sauces, p. 100. The stock will usually be chicken or fish stock. Sometimes, when specified in a recipe, chicken bouillon cubes can be used for this. Seasonings for this sauce will almost always include parsley. An egg will often be incorporated into this (see general remarks, p. 101), and frequently lemon juice will be beaten up into it first to make an egg and lemon sauce, often called Poulette. Brains, vegetables like carrots, and fish are good in this. Egg and Lemon Sauce, plain, will be seasoned only with salt.

Brown Sauce

This is for restaurants or chefs who have more time and money than the cook in the ordinary household. The closest we will come to it is a thickened beef gravy. You can thicken a gravy (the liquid the meat has cooked in) by making a brown roux and adding the gravy to it gradually as for a sauce (see general directions above). Or you can add manié "butter" (see above, also) to it, using browned flour.

Stock

The best meat stock is the liquid you have cooked meat and bones in, along with flavoring vegetables and seasonings. The same is true of chicken or fish stock. The cook in the ordinary household will not often use these ingredients just to make stock, but you often have chicken stock left from making things like Chicken Salad, or fish stock from poaching fish in a court bouillon (see p. 58). Beef stock, though, is usually some sort of compromise.

Stocks are primarily used as the basis of soups and sauces. Deliciously flavored soups and sauces can be made from the chicken or fish stocks mentioned above. Often, however, we will have to make do with second stock or substitutes.

Second stock is made from bones, scraps, skin, etc., of meat or chicken which has already been cooked. This doesn't sound like much but it can be the basis for excellent soups, and some sauces which are sufficiently flavored with other things (like egg and lemon). Always save the bones, scraps and skin and boil them in water to cover, along with a carrot, an onion and a stalk of celery. Parsley, thyme, bay leaf, clove, garlic, and pepper will improve the flavor. (Omit the garlic in making second chicken stock.) Don't add salt until you are ready to use the stock. You may also want to boil the second stock down rapidly before using, to strengthen the flavor. Strain and refrigerate stock until needed.

Substitutions will usually be stock made from bouillon cubes. Chicken bouillon cubes make stock that is frequently useful (try not to use it unless specified in recipes, though). I often use it when I make soups out of leftovers, or heat over vegetables in a thickened sauce. For the latter I often dissolve a chicken bouillon cube in ¼ cup water, fill up the cup with milk, and use that as the liquid for the sauce. Beef bouillon cubes, or worse still "beef flavor" bouillon cubes, make less successful substitutes, though they may be used with such strongly seasoned ingredients as vinegar, mustard, ketchup.

Other substitutes which can sometimes be useful are tomato juice, juices from cooking vegetables, leftover gravies (very good) or soups.

Salad Dressings

Mayonnaise

I think the difficulty of making mayonnaise has been greatly exaggerated. It does take a lot of oil, though, and so is not cheap. You may make it with just the egg yolk, or the whole egg. Double the rest of the ingredients if you use the whole egg.

1 egg yolk	about 1 cup salad or vegetable oil
½ teaspoon prepared mustard	lemon juice, to taste
¼ teaspoon salt	more mustard, to taste
1 tablespoon vinegar	

Put egg yolk, ½ teaspoon mustard, salt and vinegar in a bowl and mix well. You will add the oil very gradually throughout this next process. Start with 1 tablespoon oil, adding it to egg mixture in the mixing bowl, and beat with a rotary beater (a hand-operated one is fine, though an electric one is a convenience) for a minute or so. Continue beating, adding a tablespoon of oil at a time and beating well after each addition (at least 30 seconds) until you have a stiff mayonnaise. The total beating should be about 10 minutes, to be sure that it does not separate. As it gets stiff, taste for flavor and add lemon juice, starting with one teaspoon, and more mustard if needed. It will probably take about a cup of oil for 1 egg yolk to make it stiff enough. It doesn't need to be quite as stiff as commercial mayonnaise. If it separates while you are making it (it probably won't), put a new egg or egg yolk into another mixing bowl and add the separated mixture just as you added the oil above. This worked fine the one time it happened to me.

Boiled Dressing

This makes a very acceptable substitute for mayonnaise, I think, and is very easily made. It is fine for potato salad, fish and meat salads. I think I would prefer mayonnaise for chicken salad, but you might try this.

½ teaspoon salt	small pinch tarragon
½ teaspoon dry mustard	1 egg
1 tablespoon flour	2 tablespoons vinegar
generous tablespoon oil	½ cup milk
few drops Tabasco or hot sauce	

In a small saucepan combine salt, mustard and flour. Mix well, add oil, Tabasco and tarragon, and stir well again. Have a bigger shallow pan on a hot burner, with about an inch of water boiling. In a separate small bowl, beat up egg, add vinegar and mix well. Add milk and mix quickly. Add this to first mixture and put the small saucepan (the pan itself, not just the contents) in the boiling water, stirring constantly until the mixture thickens, 2 to 4 minutes. Refrigerate until ready to use.

French Dressing

Because I don't like to use so much oil, I use half oil and half vinegar for this. For ¼ cup of each, use ¼ teaspoon salt and black pepper to taste. Put it in a jar and shake it until mixed. I like to mash a clove of garlic and add to it for most uses. Shake vigorously just before using it as it separates very quickly, and pour it over the salad or whatever, through a strainer if you use the garlic.

****

X

Vegetables

****

MOST VEGETABLES are cooked in one or more of the following ways. The seasoning is the main difference. Special recipes will also be given for many vegetables, but you might think about each of these methods as you plan how to cook the vegetable(s) for your meal. Don't forget that a hearty dish like vegetables cooked with egg and milk will round out a skimpy meal, or that a lightly cooked one will suit a heavier meal better.

1. *Boiled.* Bring to a boil enough water to cover the vegetable, and add salt. Add vegetable and bring back to a boil. Simmer, covered, until vegetable is tender, usually 10 to 20 minutes, though some types of green leafy vegetables have to cook longer. Drain off water and save for stock. Dress vegetable with margarine, if it hasn't been cooked with some fat, and pepper. Serve hot.

This is a good method for strong-tasting vegetables like cabbage and turnips, and dark green leafy vegetables, otherwise it is more often used as a preliminary to something else. Be sure to stop cooking as soon as the vegetables are tender.

2. *Creamed.* Many vegetables may be simmered in milk, just enough to cover, and seasoned with salt and pepper. This is an excellent way to cook them because they do not lose as many vitamins and minerals as they do when cooked in water. They also take a shorter time to cook, and they are delicious cooked this way too. When the vegetables are cooked, you may cream them by adding manié "butter" (use 3 tablespoons margarine and 2 table-

spoons flour, see p. 101) to the vegetables and milk. Continue simmering until sauce is thickened. Dark green leafy vegetables may make the milk curdle, so cream them by the following method.

Leafy green vegetables, or strong ones like cabbage, should be seasoned only with salt and boiled in water first (see recipe no. 1, above) and then drained and added to a cream sauce (p. 102). You will often wish to sauté onions in the margarine until soft before adding the flour to make the roux.

Variation: Sauté bacon (ends and pieces are fine for this), cut in 1-inch pieces, until nearly crisp. Pour off excess fat, add onions and sauté until onions are soft. Then add flour to make a roux and finish making the cream sauce.

3. *Simmered in Margarine.* Chopped onions may be sautéed in the margarine before the main vegetable is added. Then cut or slice the vegetable into ½ to 1-inch pieces if it is large, while the margarine is melting and the onions, if used, are sautéing. Add the main vegetable to the pot (a heavy pot is best for this). Add salt and pepper, cover and let cook slowly until vegetables are tender, 10 to 30 minutes, depending on type and quantity of vegetable. The water that sticks to the vegetables after washing them is enough. This is a delicious way to cook many vegetables, especially summer squash and zucchini, and cabbage too if it is fairly finely shredded.

Note: Some vegetables will be better with garlic than with onions. Sauté mashed garlic instead of the onions in the margarine and proceed as above. Drained tomatoes, or a little tomato sauce or purée can be added to this, and occasionally a little lemon juice. This is such a small amount of liquid that the vegetables can still be considered as "simmered in margarine."

4. *Stewed with Other Vegetables.* Sauté one or more of the following vegetables in margarine until soft: onions, garlic, green pepper and celery. (Or ends and pieces of bacon can be cut in 1-inch pieces, sautéed until nearly crisp, excess fat poured off, and vegetables added to sauté until soft.) Add water or other liquid (often tomato) and bring to a boil. Add main vegetable. Simmer until vegetable is tender, usually 10 to 20 minutes. If tomatoes

are to be added, it is usually well to put them in when the main vegetable is nearly tender. Otherwise the acid in them adds substantially to the cooking time. Let stand a few minutes for flavors to blend.

Variation: Vegetables Creole. Sauté onions, green pepper and garlic with bacon or in bacon grease. When soft, add 1½ cups canned tomatoes (for 1 10-ounce package frozen vegetable), ½ to 1 teaspoon chili powder, good pinch ground cloves, salt and pepper. Simmer as above. Filé powder may be added after dish has completely finished cooking (it gets ropy if cooked).

5. *Vegetables Lyonnaise.* A simple way to cook these is to boil them (see recipe no. 1) until they are barely done, drain them (saving liquid for soup or stock), and then toss them in margarine, in which you have sautéed several onions, halved and sliced. I like this with a lot of pepper. Other seasonings may be added. Toss and heat in margarine with onions or other seasonings about 10 to 15 minutes for flavors to blend.

Variations: Using the same method as for vegetables Lyonnaise, substitute garlic for the onions; or to margarine and either onion or garlic add tomato sauce, paste or purée, and toss drained vegetable in this.

6. *Baked with Egg and Milk.* Boil the vegetable according to recipe no. 1. For 2 to 3 cups of the cooked vegetable, beat up 2 eggs and add about 1½ cups milk and ¼ teaspoon salt. Put 2 tablespoons margarine, cut into thin slices, in the bottom of a baking dish. Add the cooked vegetable. Beat eggs and milk and salt together and add. The liquid should come just to the top of the vegetable. Add more milk if necessary, tilting the dish back and forth to mix the milk in. Bake in a 350° oven until set and a bit browned, about 45 minutes. This is particularly good with cabbage or summer squash, and is also a good way to use them when they are left over.

7. *Marinated, or Vegetables à la Grecque.* Many vegetables are good marinated, that is, simmered until just done in a marinade, and allowed to cool in it. They will still be a little crisp when they are done because of the acid. They are served at room temperature

(about 70°), drained, with a little of the marinade dribbled over them, and fresh parsley or chervil (fresh or dried) sprinkled over them. The marinade is usually several tablespoons of oil, the juice of a lemon or 2 tablespoons of vinegar, ½ teaspoon coriander seeds, 2 teaspoons parsley, pinch of thyme and pinch of salt, bay leaf, a stalk of celery with cut-up leaves, a very little tarragon or a few fennel seeds, and water to cover. Carrots, eggplant cut in small fingers and okra are good cooked this way. Artichokes, asparagus, leeks, fennel are said to be good cooked this way too, if you happen to have any.

8. *Cooking Frozen Vegetables.* Many of these need very little cooking indeed. For spinach, green peas and corn, I melt margarine in a small frying pan, turn heat to high, add vegetable, salt and pepper, and cook, covered, until vegetables are completely heated through (watch carefully, of course). That is all there is to it. Peas and corn can be put in the pan still frozen but spinach should be thawed first. The whole thing will take less than 5 minutes. If you have forgotten to thaw the spinach, put frozen spinach and margarine over low to medium heat and let them heat slowly, turning up heat as the moisture oozes out.

French-cut snap beans are cooked much the same way as peas and corn. They will need to simmer a few minutes after heating, however, up to 10 minutes, depending on how soft you want them. I like them just going off crisp. Add just enough water to keep them from sautéing, again depending on how long you want them to cook.

For most other frozen vegetables I just follow directions on the box, if I am simmering them in water. If you are boiling green leafy vegetables before creaming them, season them only with salt.

Beans, see Snap Beans.

Cabbage

To cook or serve raw, cut the cabbage into quarters. Cut out the core and discard it. Then shred it, or chop it coarsely, or just cut each quarter lengthwise twice.

Baked Cabbage

Chop cabbage coarsely and cook according to recipe no. 6, p. 108.

Boiled Cabbage

Cut each quarter lengthwise twice and cook according to recipe no. 1, p. 106.

Cabbage Cooked in Margarine

Shred cabbage fairly finely and cook according to recipe no. 3, p. 107, seasoned only with salt and pepper.

Cabbage French Style

Cut each quarter lengthwise twice, and cook according to recipe no. 2, p. 106 (variation), using 1 tablespoon flour and ½ cup milk for the Cream Sauce (see p. 102).

Creamed Cabbage

Cut each quarter lengthwise twice and cook according to directions for leafy green vegetables in recipe no. 2, p. 106, making 2 cups cream sauce (p. 102) for a large head of cabbage. Season with a little Worcestershire sauce, or a little dill, or a little mustard.

Polish Cabbage

Chop or grate the cabbage fine and cook according to recipe no. 4 (p. 107). Simmer in ½ cup water until nearly done and add ½ to 1 cup canned tomatoes. Thicken with manié "butter," p. 101.

Slaw My Way

½ large head cabbage
⅔ cup milk
3 tablespoons vinegar
2 to 4 tablespoons boiled dressing
  (p. 105)

1 teaspoon horseradish
½ to 1 teaspoon celery seed

Add vinegar to milk and let it stand to curdle. Shred the cabbage or chop fairly fine. Put the cabbage in a bowl and add boiled dressing and horseradish and mix well. Now pour the milk, which should be nicely curdled by this time, over the whole thing. Sprinkle celery seed over it if desired. Toss well. Serve cold, but not too cold.

Colcannon (cabbage, parsnips optional, and mashed potatoes), see p. 113.

Carrots

Before cooking carrots, or before serving them raw, you must scrape them to get off the thin skin and remaining bits of dirt. A vegetable peeler is best for this. If recipe calls for cooked carrots, cut according to directions and boil in just enough salted water to cover, until tender. For big carrots, about 20 minutes.

Creamed Carrots

Scrape and simmer in milk according to recipe no. 2, p. 106. Season with chervil or parsley, or nutmeg.

Carrots Lyonnaise

Scrape and cook according to recipe no. 5, p. 108, heating carrots with onions sautéed in margarine and seasoned with ¼ teaspoon thyme and a bay leaf, and pepper.

Marinated Carrots

Use small carrots, scraped, or scrape and cut large carrots into slices lengthwise. Cook according to recipe no. 7 (p. 108), adding a garlic clove, mashed, to the marinade.

Minted Carrots

4 to 6 large cooked carrots, halved and quartered
3 tablespoons margarine, melted

handful mint leaves, chopped, or ¼ teaspoon dried mint leaves
½ teaspoon sugar

Add mint to melted margarine and let stand a minute or two. Put carrots in a greased baking dish, pour margarine and mint over them, sprinkle sugar over all and bake at 400° for 15 minutes. They may be reheated in margarine and mint and sugar on a low burner instead of in the oven unless it is going anyway. Toss occasionally.

Carrots Poulette

4 to 6 large cooked carrots, halved and quartered
cooking broth
2 tablespoons margarine
2 tablespoons flour
1 cup chicken stock or milk

1 egg, beaten
1 teaspoon lemon juice
1 teaspoon parsley
1 teaspoon chopped chives (optional)

Boil cooking broth down to ½ cup. Make a thin sauce with margarine, flour, milk and the ½ cup broth (see recipe no. 2, p. 106). Beat up egg and lemon juice in a bowl and incorporate (see p. 101) into the sauce. Add carrots, parsley and chives. Taste for salt. Reheat but do not boil.

Carrots Vichy

4 to 6 large carrots, halved and quartered
2 tablespoons margarine
½ cup water

1 teaspoon sugar
¼ teaspoon salt
parsley

Put carrots, margarine, water, sugar and salt in a large frying pan and bring to a boil. Simmer, uncovered, until water has boiled away. Then let carrots sauté slowly in the margarine already in the pan until they are lightly browned. Sprinkle with parsley.

Turnips may be cooked this way too.

Colcannon

This is cooked cabbage, parsnips cooked and mashed (optional), and mashed potatoes, all mashed up together with margarine and a little onion juice. I usually skip the parsnips and I blush to say I use instant mashed potatoes (the only convenience food I use). Boil the cabbage in just enough water to cover and 2 tablespoons margarine, grate in a little onion juice, and as soon as it is tender, add the instant potatoes until you get it to the desired consistency. This is very good.

Corn

Corn needs very little cooking. Fresh corn in season is delightful. It is much, much better if you can get it directly from a farmer. My mother used to warn me never to buy corn unless I was sure that it had been gathered that very day. To cook corn on the cob, be sure all the husks and corn silk are removed. Have a large pot of unsalted boiling water ready. Drop in the ears of corn, cut in half if you wish, and let them boil 4 minutes. They are ready to serve. Each person should salt his own and spread margarine on it (them). See p. 109 for cooking frozen corn, a fairly good substitute.

Corn O'Brien

Cook frozen corn, see recipe no. 8, p. 109. Sauté chopped green pepper and pimiento or sweet red pepper in margarine before adding corn.

Corn Fritters

2½ cups corn, fresh or frozen and thawed
¾ cup flour
1 teaspoon baking powder
½ teaspoon salt
2 eggs, separated
½ cup milk
pepper
oil or vegetable fat for frying

Sift together dry ingredients into a bowl. Add corn to this and mix well to coat the corn. In a separate bowl, beat the egg yolks. Add to the corn mixture and mix well. Add milk gradually to the corn mixture. In a third bowl (corn fritters are really worth all these bowls to wash) beat egg whites with a rotary beater until stiff but not dry (see p. 131). Fold egg whites gently into the corn mixture. Drop by tablespoonfuls into the hot oil or fat, just under smoking heat (380° if electric pan), and fry on both sides until nicely browned, about 3 to 5 minutes in all.

Leafy Green Vegetables

Spinach recipes will be found on p. 119. Other leafy green vegetables like kale, mustard greens, turnip greens and collards are generally boiled according to recipe no. 1, p. 106. They are usually boiled with bacon (ends and pieces are fine for this) or salt pork, and salt and pepper, preferably red pepper. This is the Southern method and I like it. The old recipes tell you to boil the "greens" 1½ hours. Don't do that. You may, if you like the pork cooked a long time, start boiling that before you add the green vegetables, perhaps as much as 30 minutes earlier. Then add the vegetables and cook until they are just tender, 20 to 40 minutes, depending on age and kind of greens. Season them near the end of the cooking time and be cautious with the salt, but prodigal with the pepper! If you are using frozen vegetables, follow package directions for the time.

If you are cooking fresh vegetables of this kind they will have to be washed carefully. It takes a lot of these to make enough for a meal; one recipe I have calls for a peck (8 quarts). They do cook down a lot. Put them in a large pot and fill it with cold water. Swish them around, and drain into a large colander. Rinse pot out and repeat twice (three times in all). Rinse pot out one more time and you are ready to cook them, as above.

These vegetables may be creamed. Boil as above first but season only with salt. Drain. Add vegetable to a cream sauce (p. 102) while it is bubbling. The sauce may be flavored with Tabasco or hot pepper sauce and a teaspoon of prepared mustard. If you would like to make a substantial dish out of this, grate ½ to ¾ cup of cheese. Put half of it in the creamed vegetable and stir well, and sprinkle the rest over the top.

Okra

Okra Creole

Cook according to recipe no. 4, variation, p. 108.

Okra and Tomatoes

Cook an equal quantity of these together. Add some sugar, about 1 teaspoon for 1 10-ounce package frozen okra (thawed and drained), and simmer tomatoes (canned), okra, sugar, salt and pepper together, covered, 20 to 30 minutes. If you like filé powder, add a sprinkling after the cooking has stopped. Filé powder should never be cooked.

Stewed Okra

1 10-ounce pkg. frozen okra	1 large clove garlic, mashed
oil for frying	¼ teaspoon salt
1 onion, coarsely chopped	½ teaspoon coriander seeds
½ cup canned tomatoes	pinch sugar
juice of 1 lemon	pepper

Fry okra in ⅛ inch oil until just tender. Add onions and fry until golden. Meanwhile put tomatoes and lemon juice in another pan on low heat. Mash garlic, salt and coriander seeds together and add to the second pan, along with pepper and a little water if needed. When okra is tender, take it up along with the onions with a slotted spoon and add to the tomato mixture. Cook together 5 minutes or so. Let stand 10 minutes before serving, for flavors to blend.

Green Peas

I always use frozen peas, if not canned. I have seldom had good fresh peas, though I know it is heresy to say it. There always seem to be some hard peas among the fresh ones which spoil the whole thing, or did when I was a child. I cannot honestly remember having had any since. Cook frozen peas according to recipe no. 8, p. 109.

Green Pea and Snap Bean Salad

1-pound can medium-size green peas, drained
1 10-ounce pkg. frozen regular-cut snap beans

sauce:
½ teaspoon salt
1 teaspoon prepared mustard
1 tablespoon vinegar
2 tablespoons salad oil

Cook snap beans, seasoned only with salt, according to recipe no. 1, p. 106, and drain and cool. Put drained peas and beans in a salad bowl. Put the salt in a small bowl or cup. Add mustard to this. Add a little of the vinegar and mix well. Add the rest of vinegar gradually and then add the oil. Whip with a spoon until it is well mixed and pour immediately over vegetables. Toss and let stand 30 minutes. Serve fairly cold.

Green Pea and Potato Curry

1 cup peas, fresh or frozen
2 onions, chopped
1 clove garlic, mashed
2 tablespoons margarine
½ cup canned tomatoes
½ teaspoon turmeric

1 teaspoon salt
pinch red pepper, or 1 inch hot pepper pod
2 or more medium potatoes, cut into quarters lengthwise
2 cups water

Sauté onions and garlic in margarine until soft. Add tomatoes, turmeric, salt and pepper and cook together a few minutes. Add peas and potatoes and simmer together very slowly, covered, about 10 minutes. Add water and boil, still covered, fairly vigorously so that potatoes will thicken the stew, until potatoes are tender (20 to 30 minutes). Serve over plain boiled rice. In spite of its name, this recipe calls for no curry powder.

Potatoes

Potatoes Country Style

4 medium potatoes	1 tablespoon parsley
1 onion, sliced thin	2 tablespoons margarine
salt and pepper	¾ cup boiling water

Peel and slice potatoes about ¼ inch thick. Lay the slices in a shallow baking dish. Add onion, salt and pepper and parsley and dot with margarine. Add boiling water and bake in a 400° oven until potatoes are soft and brown. They will be crusty on top.

You may lay thin slices of pork (thin pork chops, or any thinly sliced fresh pork) on top of this. Omit margarine and season pork highly with salt and pepper. I like this very, very well.

Lyonnaise Potatoes

Cook according to recipe no. 5 (p. 108), using only onions sautéed in margarine.

Aunt Lou's Potato Salad

This is rock bottom potato salad and is my favorite kind. Put potatoes, cut in ¾-inch cubes roughly, in boiling water to cover. Simmer, covered, until just soft, about 20 minutes. Drain and cool in the kitchen (not in refrigerator) for 30 minutes or so until about lukewarm. Chop very fine 1 teaspoon to 1 tablespoon onion, depending on amount of potatoes, just enough to flavor, and put into a mixing bowl. Add potatoes and enough mayonnaise to moisten. Mix carefully. If you mix this too hot or too vigorously, you will have a mush, which I don't like. I like the potato cubes firm, with just a little potato mushed off into the mayonnaise. Chill. Make a lot of this. People will eat a lot, and you can ease up on more expensive items.

This can also be made with Boiled Dressing (p. 105) or French Dressing (p. 105), and is good with these. I like mayonnaise better.

Scalloped Potatoes

Slice 1 medium-size potato for each person. Slice 1 or 2 onions thin. Put a layer of potatoes in a greased baking dish. Add onion, salt and pepper to taste, sprinkle flour over it (about 1 tablespoon for an ordinary-sized dish), and dot with margarine. Repeat these layers until potatoes are used up. Fill the dish nearly to the top of the potatoes with milk. Bake at 350° about 45 minutes, until potatoes are done. This is extremely good, and can be the largest part of the meal.

Stewed Potatoes

Potatoes may be stewed in a sauce made with beef stock and vinegar, or one made with onions and paprika and vinegar. For the first, make a sauce (see p. 100) with 4 tablespoons margarine, 4 tablespoons flour, 2 cups beef stock (may be made with bouillon cubes) and 2 tablespoons vinegar. For the second, sauté minced onions and 2 teaspoons paprika and then make a thinner sauce by adding 2 tablespoons flour and 2 cups water (see p. 100). Add 4 tablespoons vinegar and 1 bay leaf, bruised. Simmer sliced potatoes in either of these about 45 minutes. Season with salt and pepper.

Snap Beans

Snap Beans Maître d'Hôtel

Cook French-cut snap beans according to recipe no. 3, p. 107, adding a little water so that they simmer instead of sautéing (snap beans don't ooze much water). Flavor after 5 minutes with parsley and lemon juice.

Snap Bean and Green Pea Salad

See Green Pea and Snap Bean Salad, p. 116.

Armenian Snap Beans

Cook according to recipe no. 4, p. 107. Sauté onions in oil and then simmer beans in canned tomatoes a long time, an hour or more.

Creamed Snap Beans

Simmer regular cut snap beans in milk according to recipe no. 2, p. 106. Flavor with a pinch of savory and some black pepper.

Southern Boiled Snap Beans

See directions for leafy green vegetables (p. 107) for this. Cook with salt pork and red pepper.

Spinach

I always use either frozen or canned spinach. Canned spinach tastes canned, but it is not bad, really, so it is a good emergency vegetable to have on hand. Poached eggs on canned spinach make a pretty good lunch.

See directions for leafy green vegetables, p. 107, in case someone gives you some fresh spinach. A great armful cooks down to nearly nothing. Don't cook it in much water, though, or very long. Cook frozen spinach according to recipe no. 8, p. 109.

Creamed Spinach

Cook frozen spinach, then follow recipe no. 2, for leafy green vegetables (p. 107). Flavor with ⅛ teaspoon grated nutmeg.

Spinach with Garlic

Cook frozen spinach according to recipe no. 5, p. 108. Sauté mashed garlic in 2 tablespoons margarine and toss spinach in this.

Sprinkle with pepper. You may flavor it with lemon juice; it is quite good either with or without the lemon.

Spinach with Tomato and Onion

Cook as for spinach with garlic, substituting onion for garlic. Flavor with tomato paste, purée or sauce, to taste.

Yellow, or Summer Squash

This is close kin to zucchini and the round white squash (cymblings). They may be cooked in many of the same ways. Zucchini is especially good simmered in margarine, and cymblings are good baked with egg and milk. To cook squash, cut a bit off either end, and slice about ¼ inch thick. If the squash is large it may be quartered first.

Baked Squash

Prepare as above and cook according to recipe no. 6, p. 108.

Squash and Onions, Boiled

Prepare squash as above, add sliced onions, and cook according to recipe no. 1, p. 106. I don't think this is as good as the following recipe, but it has an appeal of its own and you may want to try it.

Squash and Onions, Cooked in Margarine

Add squash, prepared as above, to onions sautéed in a good deal of margarine and cook according to recipe no. 3, p. 107. This is one of my favorite vegetable dishes.

Squash with Tomato

This is also extremely good. Cook as above, seasoned with 2 tablespoons tomato purée or paste or sauce, and the juice of half a lemon.

Sweet Potatoes

Baked Sweet Potatoes

All you do to bake these is to put them in the oven, unwashed. Do not prick them, or they will leak. You may bake them at 300° for 2 hours or at 400° for 1 hour, whichever suits the rest of your meal. These are very good, and add valuable vitamins and fiber to your diet. Bake some extra ones while the oven is going, to make fritters or a pie (p. 126) another day. Or you can just slice them when cold (and peeled) and fry them plain in ⅛ inch of bacon grease, preferably, until nicely browned. They are very good any of these ways.

Sweet Potato Fritters

3 or 4 large sweet potatoes, baked
  and peeled
4 tablespoons margarine
3 tablespoons flour

salt to taste
fat for frying, preferably bacon
  grease

Mash potatoes well. Add melted margarine, flour, salt and pepper, and mix thoroughly. Heat frying pan as for pancakes (380° if electric) with fat about ¼ inch deep. Put a tablespoon of potato mixture in at a time, patting each fritter down with a spoon. Fry until nicely browned, and turn over and do the same.

Turnips

Turnips are delicious if they are not *too* old (though they are edible even then) and are not overcooked. They should be cooked until they are just transparent. If they are thinly sliced, it probably won't take more than 10 minutes.

Turnip Fritters

3 cups cooked turnips (see recipe no. 1, p. 106)
3 eggs, beaten
1 teaspoon salt

1 cup flour
1 cup milk
fat for frying, preferably oil or vegetable shortening

Mash turnips, drain off excess liquid and add the rest of the ingredients except the fat. Have the fat, ⅛ inch deep, almost smoking in a frying pan (400° if electric). Put the turnip mixture in by the tablespoonful, and flatten each fritter. Fry until brown on both sides, about 4 minutes in all.

Mashed Turnips

Peel and slice turnips thin and cook according to recipe no. 1, p. 106. Drain and mash in a colander to remove moisture. Melt margarine in the pan, add turnips, salt and pepper if needed, and a little milk, but don't let it get runny. Serve hot.

Turnips Vichy

Cook as for Carrots Vichy, p. 112.

****

XI

Desserts

****

THIS IS A VERY PERSONAL collection of recipes. Desserts should not play a large part in your plans when times are hard because they do little to round out your diet. But there are festive occasions when a dessert is really called for, and here are my two favorite cakes and icings, my three favorite pies and pastry, Chocolate Soufflé, which my mother always used to have for me when I came home from out of town, and two lowly but delicious sweets, Scotch Shortbread and Molasses Johnny Cake. These last two are very inexpensive; you won't have to wait for a special occasion to serve them.

Helen's Cake

This is my very favorite cake for icing. The recipe given me by my friend and great cake maker called for ½ pound butter, 2 cups sugar, 5 eggs, 3 cups flour, 1 tablespoon baking powder, 1 cup milk and 1½ teaspoons vanilla. This makes a noble cake, with three 9-inch layers. She used to bring my husband and me this cake iced with boiled chocolate or caramel icing, and our friends thought us very fortunate, as indeed we were. Now I make a smaller cake as follows:

1¾ cups flour	3 eggs
1¾ teaspoons baking powder	generous ½ cup milk, 5 ounces
5 ounces margarine	scant teaspoon vanilla
1½ cups sugar	

Sift together flour and baking powder. Cream margarine, add sugar gradually, and cream together until light and fluffy. Add eggs one at a time, beating after each one. Now add flour mixture alternately with the milk, adding vanilla with the second half of the milk. Divide batter between two 8-inch pans, 1½ inches deep, which have been greased and floured. Bake at 350° about 30 minutes, or until done (begins to shrink away from the pan, or a knife stuck in it will come out clean).

1-2-3-4 Cake

This is a traditional cake and is rich and delicious served perfectly plain, baked in a large tube pan.

8 ounces margarine (1 cup)	1 tablespoon baking powder
2 cups sugar	1 teaspoon salt
4 eggs	1 teaspoon vanilla
3 cups flour	1 cup milk

Mix cake like the one above, adding salt with the flour. Put batter in a greased and floured tube pan, 3-quart capacity, and bake at 350° for one hour, or until done (see recipe above).

Caramel Icing

This is real caramel icing and is much better than the quick kinds. I like it a little better with dark brown sugar, but light brown may be used. The dark is prettier and a tiny bit stronger in flavor.

3 cups brown sugar (1 pound plus about ⅓ cup)
1 cup milk

3 tablespoons margarine
1 teaspoon vanilla

Put all ingredients in a large saucepan (at least 2½ quarts) and stir constantly over low heat until sugar and margarine are melted. Raise heat to medium and cook, uncovered, until it reaches the soft ball stage (see below). If you have a candy-icing thermometer, it will read somewhere between 230° and 238°. If it goes too slowly, turn up the heat a little. When it reaches the soft ball stage, take off the heat and cool until you can keep your hand on the bottom of the pan. Beat until it is the right consistency to spread. (It pours, but does not run.)

"Soft Ball Stage." Have a cup of cold water handy when you are making icing. When you think it is nearly ready, drop a few drops into the water, and try to gather it up into a ball. It is ready when it gathers up into a coherent ball, but the ball is still soft, or fairly soft.

Chocolate Icing, Boiled

This is not particularly troublesome, but it is tricky, and it may take you several tries before you get it just right. It is better to overcook it a little, because you can thin it if necessary, than to undercook it, because then it will run off the cake and you can't do anything about it but scoop up the icing and eat it. I am including it, though, because this, and the recipe for caramel icing above, are among the best sweet things in the world to eat. It is definitely worth the effort to learn how to do this. It is unbelievably good on a fairly substantial yellow cake, like Helen's cake.

2½ ounces unsweetened chocolate   ⅛ teaspoon salt
2 cups sugar   3 tablespoons margarine
⅞ cup milk   1 teaspoon vanilla

Put chocolate, sugar, and milk in a saucepan and stir constantly over low heat until dissolved. Turn heat to medium and boil, uncovered, about 9 to 10 minutes, until the soft ball stage (see page 124) is reached, about 234°. Remove from the stove and add margarine. Let cool until you can keep your hand on the bottom of the pan. Add vanilla and beat it until it is hard enough to spread.

Until you get the hang of this, have a container, large enough to put the icing pan in, ready with hot water to the depth of about 1 inch or more. Also have some hot milk handy. If the icing gets too hard, or if it begins to harden too quickly, put the icing pan in the hot water, and add 2 tablespoons of the hot milk. Continue to add hot milk, one tablespoon at a time, beating all the while, until it is spreadable.

Lemon Pie

This is the lemon pie I grew up on and is, in my opinion, vastly superior to the usual "lemon chiffon pie" with meringue.

3 eggs, beaten   grated rind of 1 lemon
1 cup sugar   2 tablespoons melted margarine
juice of 2 lemons

Add sugar to eggs and beat thoroughly. Add lemon juice and lemon rind, being careful to wash and dry the lemon you are going to grate. Grate only the yellow part of the rind. Stir in margarine. Bake on unbaked pastry shell (see page 126) in a 9-inch tin for about an hour at 325°.

Pecan Pie

3 eggs   ⅛ teaspoon salt
1¾ cups light brown sugar   3 tablespoons melted margarine
  (packed in measuring cup)   1 cup pecan meats, coarsely
¾ cup granulated sugar   broken
1 teaspoon vanilla

Beat eggs until light and add sugars gradually. Add vanilla and salt and then the melted margarine. Mix well. Line a 9-inch pie tin with pastry (see below). Sprinkle unbaked pastry with half the nuts. Pour in egg mixture and sprinkle the rest of the nuts on top. Bake at 350° about an hour. Reduce heat to 300° for the last 20 minutes.

Sweet Potato Pie

This is one of my favorite delicacies from the South. Leave it as it is — don't mess it up with a lot of spices.

⅔ cup cooked sweet potatoes	¼ teaspoon salt
2 eggs, beaten	scant ½ cup milk
⅔ cup sugar	⅓ cup margarine, melted

Mash the cooked sweet potatoes. (Boiled is all right, but baked is better.) Add beaten eggs, sugar, and salt and mix well. Add milk gradually to make a smooth batter. Add melted margarine and beat it in thoroughly. Line a 9-inch pie tin with pastry (see below), pour in mixture and bake in 400° oven 30 to 40 minutes, or until pie is set (knife will come out clean).

Pastry

You will find below a very rough and ready recipe. It is easy and needs no chilling. I find the time to make this, and I never could when I thought I had to make a fancier one. I think this is just fine, and you can make it and put it in the pan(s) in 20 minutes. This amount of dough will be enough to line two shallow 9-inch pie tins, or make lining and top for one pie, or make a good many tarts.

2 cups flour	pinch salt
4 ounces margarine (or better: 2 ounces margarine, 2 ounces lard)	cold water, less than ¼ cup

Sift flour and salt, and rub the fat (p. 130) into this. Add cold water, a little at a time, and gather up the dough in your hands into a solid ball. This is a gradual process; at first just a little will stick together and then as you add the water more and more will stick, until you have the solid ball. Use just as little water as possible and still have the dough a solid mass.

To roll out: put the dough on a floured board and flour the rolling pin. Divide the dough into appropriate amounts and roll each separately. Roll the dough gently, flouring the board (lift up dough for this) and rolling pin as often as necessary to keep dough from sticking to them. Dough should be thin, $\frac{1}{16}$ inch or less, and maneuvred into the shape you will need. When it is thin enough, and about the right shape (in practice you will roll it out a bit larger than needed because you cannot get it into exactly the right shape, and then you trim the edges), put the rolling pin at the top of the pastry, hold the top edge of the dough on the rolling pin, roll the pin back toward you, peeling the dough up from the board. Pick up the pin with both hands, with the dough hanging down on both sides. Hold it over the pie tin. Roll dough off the rolling pin into the pie tin. Gently press dough into the tin, working from the outside in so as not to put a strain on the dough, now pretty thin. Trim the edges, using the trimming to patch up any errors of judgment. Be sure there are no air holes between pastry and tin. Prick bottom with a fork several times.

The pies in this chapter don't have tops, but if you are making a pie that does require a top, like a meat pie, the dough for it is rolled out in the same way, making sure that it is enough to cover the pie, with some to spare. When you have finished rolling it out, but before lifting it up off the board, wet the edges of the bottom crust (this will make the top stick to it — be sure that the crust for the bottom has a flat edge you can stick the top to). Then lift the crust up and ease it onto the pie. Crimp down the edge of the top onto the edge of the bottom with the tines of a fork. Prick the top crust 6 or 8 times with a fork, or cut a small hole in the middle, for the steam to escape.

Chocolate Soufflé

2 tablespoons margarine $\frac{1}{3}$ cup sugar
2 tablespoons flour   3 eggs, separated
$\frac{3}{4}$ cup milk   pinch salt
2 tablespoons hot water

Make a thick cream sauce with margarine, flour and milk (p. 102). Melt chocolate with water in a small saucepan and add to the cream sauce. Add vanilla. Beat egg yolks and sugar until light. Add chocolate mixture to eggs and sugar. This much may be done 2 or 3 hours before you wish to serve it. At the last minute before cooking beat egg whites with rotary or electric beater until they are stiff but not dry (will hold a peak when you take the beater out). Fold (see p. 129) into the chocolate mixture. Bake at 375° for 45 minutes.

Scotch Shortbread

8 ounces margarine	2½ cups sifted flour
10 tablespoons sugar	

Cream margarine. Add sugar, 2 tablespoons at a time. Beat until light and fluffy. Stir in flour. Roll out $\frac{5}{16}$ to $\frac{3}{8}$ inch thick. Cut in strips about $\frac{5}{16}$ inch wide and 2 to 2½ inches long. These should look a little like square cigarettes. Bake at 300° for 25 minutes. Leave room between each one for them to spread a little. These are *very* good, excellent to serve with tea.

Molasses Johnny Cake

I think this is sweet enough to make a good dessert, but it is not very sweet and could be served with the meal.

1 egg	¼ cup molasses
¼ cup sugar	1 cup buttermilk
¼ teaspoon salt	1 cup flour
1 teaspoon soda	1 cup cornmeal

Beat egg and sugar together and add salt. Dissolve soda in 1 tablespoon water and add to molasses. Stir until it foams. Combine with egg mixture. Add the rest of the ingredients and mix thoroughly. Bake at 400° for 30 minutes. This is utterly delicious when hot. Toast any left over and spread with margarine.

Notes

****
I HAVE CHOSEN these few notes to put here because this information is referred to throughout the book.

Crumbs. Many recipes call for soft crumbs, toast crumbs or toasted and buttered crumbs. Soft crumbs are made from fresh bread. One slice of bread will make about ½ cup crumbs. The easiest way to make them is to grate them. Rub bread slices gently over the next to finest side of the grater and you will get mostly nice crumbs. Pick out the big pieces that always fall off and rub them together between your palms until they crumb nicely.

For toast crumbs you may put slices of dry toast on a clean counter or cookie sheet and roll them with a rolling pin until you get fine crumbs. Or you can use the grater for slices of toast too. This is a bit simpler unless you want to make a lot of crumbs. One slice of toast makes about ¼ cup crumbs.

To make toasted and buttered crumbs, make toast crumbs as above. Melt margarine in a small saucepan or frying pan and add toast crumbs. Stir until all crumbs are well coated.

Egg Whites. To beat up egg whites, put them in a bowl with a pinch of salt. Beat with wire whisk, rotary beater, or electric beater. It has been a long time since I've beat them with a wire whisk but it can be done. The other two are easier. Beat until they foam up and become fairly stiff. Pick up the beater. If the peaks stand up straight they are ready. If they fold over, beat a while longer. To fold beaten egg whites into anything, put them on top of the other mixture. With a large spoon cut down through both mixtures, bring it back up gently and fold or turn the two mixtures over a bit. The idea is to incorporate the two mixtures without breaking the little air cells you have beaten into the egg whites. If you stir the mixture, you will stir out a lot of air. Just keep cutting the spoon through the mixture and turning it over gently until everything is mixed together. The mixture should be light and airy.

Rubbing Margarine into Flour. This is different from rubbing flour into margarine, which you do for manié "butter" (see p. 101). For that you just mash them into a paste. What we are doing here is taking the first step toward making dough for biscuits, turnovers and the like, or for pastry. When you have finished you will have a light, fairly dry mixture, looking something like meal. You mix the margarine and flour, but in a special way to keep it from becoming a paste. You can buy a pastry blender for this, but it is quite easy to do it with your fingers. Have the margarine fairly soft but do not let it melt. Sift the flour and any other dry ingredients into a bowl. Add the margarine. Pinch through the margarine several times and then lift it or toss it in the flour to coat each bit with flour. Pinch it some more, and then put your fingers under the flour and lift it up so the margarine pieces will be tossed in it. Keep pinching the margarine (the pieces will get smaller and smaller) and lifting up the flour to coat the margarine, until it is the consistency of coarse meal. Never mash it or stir it or it will turn into a paste. It is really extremely easy and quick to do, though a bit difficult to describe. Rubbing any fat or shortening into flour, lard, butter, or commercial shortenings such as Crisco, is the same process. Margarine, though, is generally cheaper.

Tomatoes. In many recipes you can use canned tomatoes, tomato paste, tomato purée or tomato sauce interchangeably, depending on what you have. The most concentrated is tomato paste, to which you may add water. Several tablespoons plus a bit less than a cup of water would give much the same effect as a cup of canned tomatoes. Half a cup of either tomato purée or tomato sauce plus half a cup of water would do about the same. I like the purée better as it tastes less canned.

Until Done. This is an irritating phrase often found in cookbooks. I have tried to give an approximate time as a rule, but stoves and ingredients do vary. Except with rice and things baked I think it will be self-evident. For rice dishes, see the recipe for Boiled Rice II, p. 13. For baked dishes, insert a table knife, or stainless steel knife. If it comes out clean and dry, the baked dish should be done.

****

On Nutrition and Budgets

****

IF YOU ARE GOOD at planning and with figures, one of the best buys you can make is the Home and Garden Bulletin (No. 72), *Nutritive Value of Foods*, 41 pp. It is put out by the U.S. Department of Agriculture and is available for less than a dollar from the Superintendent of Documents, U.S. Government Printing Office, Washington, D.C. 20402. It gives the recommended daily allowances for calories, proteins, most of the vitamins and the most important minerals, and then has 35 pages listing foods and showing how much, in servings and in grams, each one contains of these elements. I wish I had a nickel for every hour I have spent poring over it; it is the basis of the food budgets given later in this chapter. It is extremely useful if you are really pinching every penny to be able to check up on how much energy and how much protein five pounds of flour will give you, for example, as compared with five pounds of rice, or beans, or sugar. You will soon see from it that flour is your best buy among these. Or you may find that while a cup of cooked mustard greens contains a lot of iron, a cup of canned green peas will give you nearly twice as much. Studying this pamphlet will amply repay you in deciding how to spend your food dollar.

Yearbook of Agriculture 1959

Comparison of Amino Acid Patterns of Common Foods

	Tryptophan	*Lysine*	*Methionine plus cystine*
FAO pattern	1	3	3
Milk, cow	1	5.5	2.4
Milk, human	1	4.0	2.5
Buttermilk	1	7.7	3.0
Cheese, Cheddar	1	5.4	2.3
Cheese, cottage	1	8.0	3.4
Cheese, cream	1	9.0	3.9
Egg	1	3.9	3.3
Beef	1	7.5	3.2
Lamb	1	6.2	2.9
Pork	1	6.3	2.8
Chicken	1	7.2	3.2
Fish	1	8.8	4.3
Heart	1	6.3	2.6
Kidney	1	4.9	2.2
Liver	1	5.0	2.4
Tongue	1	6.9	2.9
Beans, common	1	8.0	2.2
Chickpeas	1	8.5	3.4
Cowpeas, dried	1	6.8	3.0
Lentils	1	7.1	1.8
Lima beans	1	7.1	3.3
Peanuts	1	3.2	2.2
Peas, dried	1	6.9	2.4
Pigeon peas	1	13.3	4.7
Soybeans	1	4.6	2.3
Soybean milk	1	5.3	2.5
Coconut	1	4.6	4.0
Cottonseed flour	1	3.6	2.5
Sesame meal	1	1.8	5.4
Sunflower meal	1	2.5	2.6
Barley	1	2.7	2.8
Bread (4 percent dry milk solids)	1	2.5	3.8
Buckwheat flour	1	4.2	2.6
Cornmeal	1	4.7	5.2
Pearlmillet	1	1.5	1.7
Oatmeal	1	2.9	2.8
Rice	1	3.7	2.9
Rye	1	3.6	3.2
Sorghum	1	2.4	3.0
Wheat	1	2.2	3.0
Flour, white	1	1.9	2.7

	Tryptophan	Lysine	Methionine plus cystine
Corn, raw	1	5.9	5.8
Cowpeas, raw	1	6.2	...
Lima beans, raw	1	4.9	1.7
Peas, raw	1	5.7	2.3
Spinach	1	3.8	2.3
Turnip greens	1	2.8	2.1
Potatoes	1	5.0	2.1
Sweetpotatoes	1	2.7	2.0
Broccoli	1	3.9	...

Calculated from "Amino Acid Content of Foods," by Martha Louise Orr and Bernice Kunerth Watt. Home Economics Research Report No. 4, Agricultural Research Service.

Another great help is the chart on amino acid patterns which appeared in one of the yearbooks of the U.S. Department of Agriculture. I am reproducing it here because it does not appear in the *Nutritive Value of Foods*. It was calculated on the basis of "Amino Acid Content of Foods," by Martha Louise Orr and Bernice Kunerth Watt, Home Economics Research Report No. 4, Agricultural Research Service. It is over fifteen years old, but it is the work still cited in current publications. Amino acids are components of protein. All are necessary for proper nutrition and therefore for good health. Many of them can be made by the body out of other materials, but others cannot. The latter must be present, "completely formed and ready for use" in the food we eat. (Ruth Leverton, "Amino Acids," pp. 64–73 in U.S. Department of Agriculture *Yearbook*, 1959.) These are called the essential amino acids; there are eight in all, but the ones most likely to be in short supply in our diet are the three listed across the top of the chart.

There is a further refinement, however, in the body's use of amino acids in protein. It is not enough to have all the essentials represented; they must also be present in correct proportion in each meal, or the body cannot use them properly. For example, beans are high in one essential amino acid but relatively low in a second. Wheat on the other hand is low in the first but higher in the second. Neither, by itself, can be used with best efficiency as protein in the body, but eaten at the same meal they complement each other sufficiently to provide good protein. Protein providing the correct proportions of essential amino acids is called a complete protein. Animal protein such as meat, milk, eggs, fish is complete; that is, it supplies amino acids in correct proportion. But if we are not going to be able to get enough of our protein from these sources, it is important to combine other foods in such a way as to provide as complete protein as possible.

If you look at the chart you will see that the first item is "FAO (Food and Agriculture Organization of the United Nations) pattern." Studies have shown that if these three acids are roughly in this 1-3-3 proportion, other things are likely to fall together, and the amino acid requirements will have been met. Look again at the chart, and you will see that bread and milk combine to make a better ratio than bread alone, or that beans and any kind of grain make a better pattern than either alone. As we might have guessed, a peanut butter sandwich is an excellent thing, combining bread and peanuts, which again make a better pattern together than either does alone. This kind of information may become more and more important if we are forced to rely less on animal protein in our diet and more on grains, and the like. For the present, however, we should certainly try to have as much milk and other dairy products, eggs and other cheaper forms of animal protein as we can, and use this type of information mainly as a useful pointer in deciding what to have with what.

To go from the general to the specific, let us suppose that you are suddenly hit with a financial emergency. You have much less to spend than you would if you were on welfare, let us say, and there is no food in the house. If you could check the charts in the *Nutritive Value of Foods*, keeping in mind the price of the various items, you would find that the best buy for your money is flour, considering both protein content and the amount of energy you get from it (counted in calories). But if you check the amino acid patterns chart you will see that flour needs complementing if it is to provide good protein. Beans and cornmeal will do that, so you will want to include those too, especially as they are very good buys as well. You should also buy as much milk and eggs as possible, and fill out the number of calories you need with margarine and sugar. These things will have to be the basis of your meals and you should spend about 80 percent of your money on them. On this emergency budget, a good combination for a family of six for one week might be:

20 lbs. flour	2 dozen eggs
10 lbs. cornmeal	6 lbs. rice
6 lbs. beans	7 lbs. margarine
dried milk to make 12 qts.	28-oz. can baking powder

This would give you about enough calories (food energy) for six, and an acceptable level of protein with a fairly good balance (watch the amino acid patterns chart and serve the right things together). Below are two shopping lists with menus to match, the first assuming nothing on hand, and the second after stock-piling a few other foods and seasonings. The groceries listed would comprise the other 20 percent of your food money, after buying the items listed above.

For each of these two weeks I'm assuming pancakes (made with 3 cups flour, 3 eggs and melted margarine, but with water instead of milk) and café au lait (half coffee and half hot milk, with sugar to taste — very heartwarming in the morning) for breakfast every day. This will use up most of the eggs, but a good start in the morning is essential in hard times. When your budget improves, you can vary your breakfast.

Emergency Low Budget with Nothing on Hand
20% budget, after buying staples (*above*)

1 lb. coffee	1 10-oz. pkg. spinach
1 lb.-can mackerel	1 doz. oranges
3 lbs. onions	1 box salt
1 pkg. garlic buds	1 can curry powder
1 lb. carrots	

	Lunch	*Supper*
Mon.	lentils w. rice & onions, biscuits	rice w. milk and sugar, biscuits ½ orange ea.
Tues.	rice w. garlic, biscuits, milk	Great Northern bean soup w. onions and carrots, dumplings

Wed.	fried black-eyed peas, biscuits	rice w. onions, muffins
Thurs.	batterbread & biscuits	lentils w. rice and onions, hoecake
Fri.	kidney bean soup w. garlic, dumplings	rice tossed w. sautéed onions & carrots
Sat.	baked rice, hoecakes	fried pinto beans w. onions, biscuits
Sun.	kedgeree w. mackerel, onions, curry powder; spinach, hoecakes	rice w. milk & sugar, ½ orange ea.

Emergency Still But Some Things Stockpiled
20% budget, after buying staples (*above*)

4 lbs. cabbage (1 large)
3 lbs. bacon, ends & pieces
1 lb. ground beef
1-lb. can tomatoes
1 doz. oranges
3 lbs. onions
small can turmeric

beans will be:
  Great Northern (2 lbs.)
  black-eyed peas
  lentils
  kidney beans
  dried lima beans

	Lunch	*Supper*
Mon.	bean-cabbage-bacon soup, hoecakes	rice w. turmeric & garlic, biscuits, milk
Tues.	curried rice w. onions, hoecakes, milk	black-eyed peas w. bacon & onions, slaw
Wed.	lentil soup w. mint & onions, hoecakes	baked rice w. biscuits ½ orange ea.
Thurs.	rice w. onions & a few kidney beans, milk, biscuits	kidney beans w. garlic & cumin, corn bread
Fri.	dried lima beans w. coriander & garlic, biscuits	tomato pilaff w. bacon, hoecakes
Sat.	batter bread, biscuits	Great Northern bean salad, w. mint & French dressing
Sun.	cabbage-rice-ground beef casserole, biscuits	rice w. milk & sugar, ½ orange ea.

Very few people in this country have to live on budgets like this. A man on minimum wages with a wife and family of four children could do a great deal better. People living on Social Security, or even most welfare programs, can do much better than this. No one should try to live on it long. I just wanted you to see what could be done on a temporary basis with a rock bottom budget.

Here are two budgets more likely for people in this country, even people with the lowest incomes. One is calculated for a family of six and calls for a very modest expenditure. It is substantially lower than the lowest of the U.S. Department of Agriculture's four food plans (economy, low cost, moderate cost and liberal). But you will see that it is quite possible to have delicious and nourishing meals from it.

My fourth shopping list with menus is for a retired couple living exclusively on Social Security. It calls for expenditure which is a small proportion of the mean Social Security check, less than you would be allotted in food stamps on such a budget.

The starred items on these lists are ongoing things that you would be using for several weeks. It is presupposed that you would have other groceries of this nature on hand, left over from other weeks.

Family of Six

Groceries

2 lbs. sugar
dried milk for 32 qts.
*10 lbs. rice
1 chicken
1 lb. salt pork
4 lbs. cabbage
1 lb. carrots
*20 lbs. flour
3 doz. eggs
*spices, etc.

4 1-lb.-cans tomatoes
2 pkgs. froz. greens
1 pkg. froz. peas
4 lbs. margarine
1 lb. bacon
*24 oz. oil
1 lb. ground beef
*15 lbs. potatoes
*celery
1½ lbs. pork liver

*1 lb. coffee
9 1½-lb. loaves bread
3 lbs. beans
1 lb. froz. fish
2 doz. oranges
3 lbs. onions
1 lb. cheese
1 lb. sausage

	Breakfast	Lunch	Dinner
Mon.	pancakes, milk, coffee	English monkey, slaw	liver, scalloped potatoes minted carrots
Tues.	eggs and bacon (2 slices, crumbled) milk, coffee	fassoulada, biscuits	sausage pie, cabbage
Wed.	muffins, milk, coffee	chow farn, oranges	keema on rice
Thurs.	pancakes, milk, coffee	soup from keema, plus more beans	macaroni & cheese mustard greens
Fri.	muffins, milk, coffee	batter bread, oranges	baked fish espagnole, baked potatoes, creamed kale
Sat.	pancakes, milk, coffee	split pea soup, corn bread	liver fritters, grits, carrots Vichy
Sun.	eggs and crumbled bacon, milk, coffee	chicken and dumplings, marinated carrots	colcannon, hoecakes

Retired Couple

Groceries

dried milk for 12 qts.	*spices, etc.	3 1½ lb. loaves bread
1 lb. beans	*3 lbs. onions	*24 oz. oil
*5 lbs. rice	1 lb. margarine	1 lb. pork liver
1 pkg. froz. kale	*5 lbs. flour	1 doz. oranges
1 pkg. froz. spinach	*1 lb. bacon	1 lb. carrots
*2 lbs. sugar	1 lb. frozen fish	*1 lb. coffee
2 doz. eggs	*4 lb.-cans tomatoes	
1 lb. ground beef	2 lbs. cabbage	

	Breakfast	Lunch	Dinner
Mon.	pancakes, milk, coffee	tomato pilaff	macaroni & cheese, kale (½ pkg.)

Tues.	eggs & crumbled bacon, milk, coffee	Tio Pepe (⅓ lb. beans), slaw	½ lb. liver, kale grits
Wed.	cornmeal muffins, milk, coffee	fried grits w. tomato sauce & grated cheese	fish with egg and vinegar sauce, baked potatoes, cabbage sim. in margarine
Thurs.	pancakes, milk, coffee	egg & lemon soup w. broth from Wed. fish, biscuits	ground beef & rice casserole, oranges
Fri.	eggs & crumbled bacon, milk, coffee	batter bread, oranges	liver fritters, biscuits, spinach
Sat.	plain muffins, milk, coffee	lentil soup (⅓ lb.)	creamed fish on toast, carrots Vichy
Sun.	omelet, milk, coffee	chili con carne with beans on rice (⅓ lb. beans, ½ lb. ground beef)	chow farn, oranges

CONVERSION TABLE FROM
U.S. STANDARD MEASURES TO METRIC MEASURES

1 oz. = 28 grams

3½ oz. = 100 grams

8 oz. = 227 grams

1 lb. = 454 grams

1 gallon = 3.79 liters

1 quart = .95 liters or 950 milliliters

1 pint = .48 liters or 480 milliliters

1 cup (8 oz.) = .24 liters or 240 milliliters

1 tablespoon = 15 milliliters

1 teaspoon = 5 milliliters

Index

This index is ingredient oriented. Names of dishes are included, of course, but there has also been an effort to make it helpful if you are wondering how you can best use whatever you have in your pantry or refrigerator. Lists of recipes will be found as usual under the names of meats and vegetables, but also under eggs (even for recipes calling for just an egg or two), milk (where you will find chowders, for example) and such things as cheese, rice and beans, not to mention leftovers, and stocks or gravies.